THE PHOTOGRAPHER'S
PORTFOLIO DEVELOPMENT
WORKSHOP

WILLIAM NEILL

The Photographer's Portfolio Development Workshop
William Neill
www.WilliamNeill.com

Project editor: Jocelyn Howell
Project manager: Lisa Brazieal
Marketing coordinator: Katie Walker
Book interior and cover design: Aren Straiger
Layout: Kim Scott/Bumpy Design

ISBN: 978-1-68198-823-8
1st Edition (1st printing, June 2022)
© 2022 William Neill
All images © William Neill

Rocky Nook Inc.
1010 B Street, Suite 350
San Rafael, CA 94901
USA

www.rockynook.com

Distributed in the UK and Europe by Publishers Group UK
Distributed in the U.S. and all other territories by Ingram Publisher Services

Library of Congress Control Number: 2021937329

CONTENTS

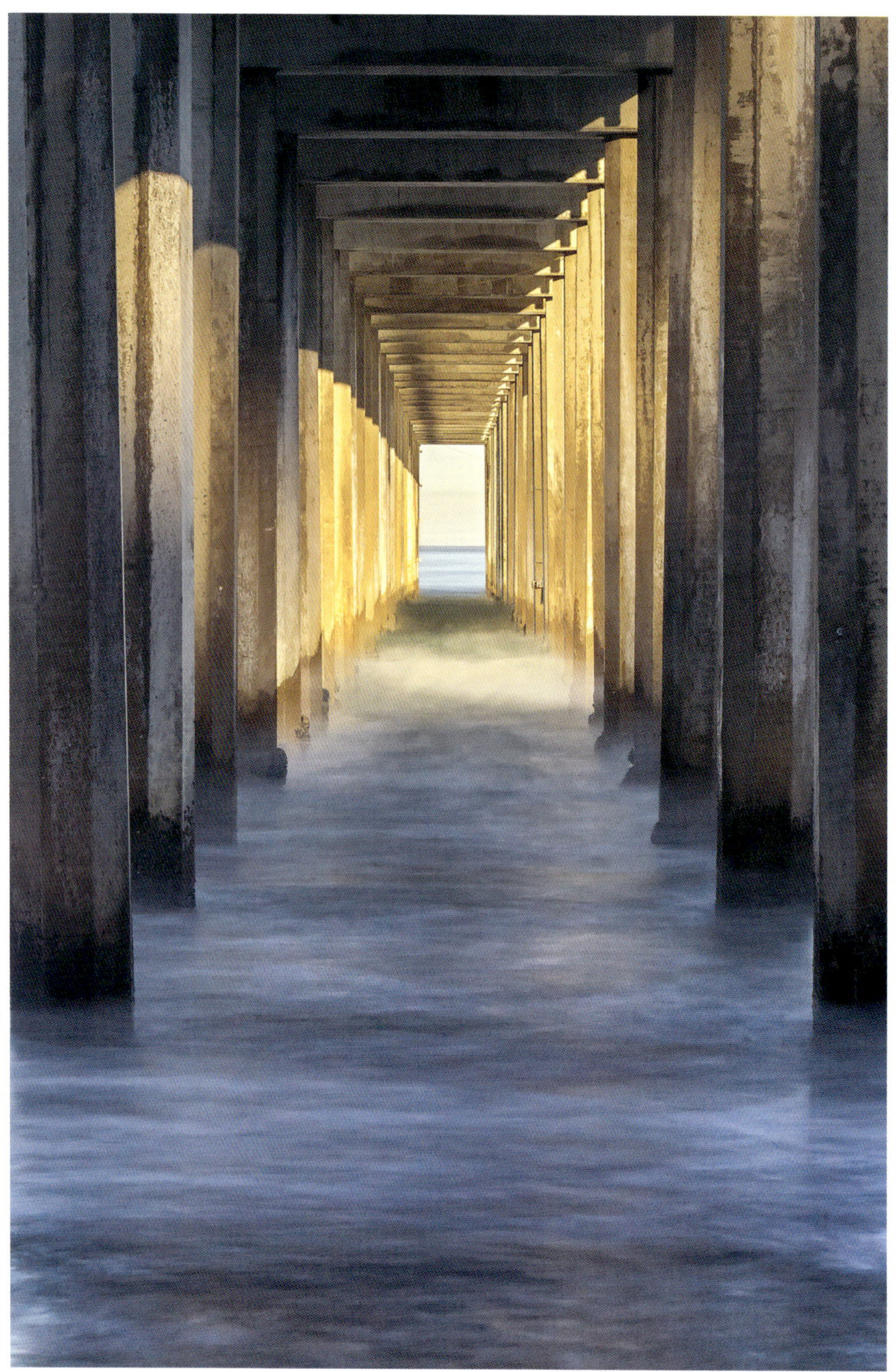

Sunrise, Scripps Pier, La Jolla, California, 2010

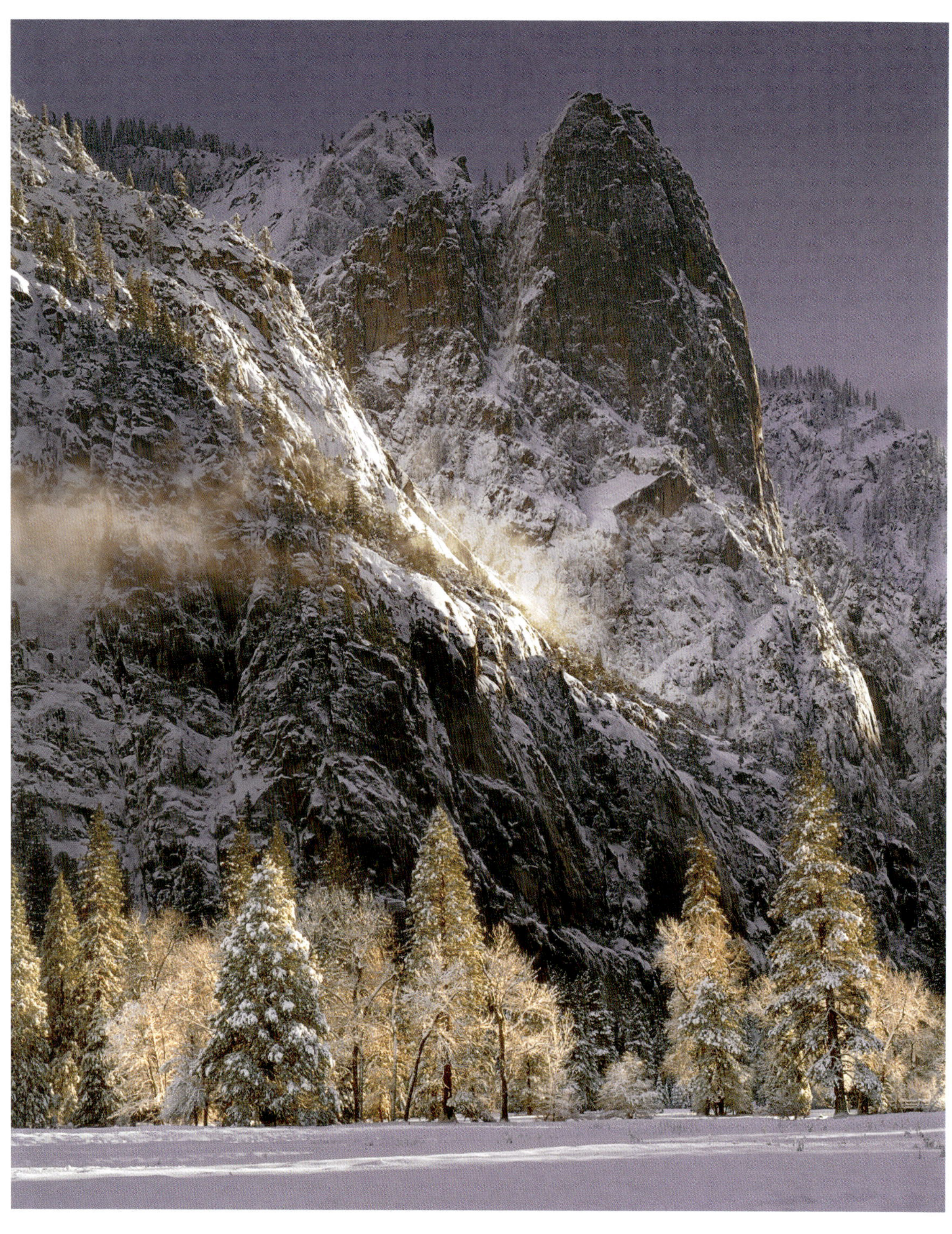

Clearing Winter Storm, Sentinel Rock, Yosemite Valley, Yosemite National Park, California, 1990

HOW TO USE THIS BOOK

This book requires you to be an active participant—it is a workshop in book form, not a book to be read through cover-to-cover in one sitting. In order to get the most out of the lessons that follow, you will need to put in the work. Just as you will not get fit simply by reading a book about fitness, you will not reap the full benefits of these lessons without actively engaging with the process and doing your best to complete the assignments. I will guide you through this process and share insights I have gained through years of personal practice and teaching workshops, and as you complete the assignments, you will develop your own thoughts and processes that can be practiced again and again. Simply put, the true value here is the time and effort that you commit to developing your portfolio.

These lessons were originally written for an eight-week online course. Although that course had a weekly progression of lessons, assignments, and feedback from the instructor, this workshop can easily be followed in a similar manner. I suggest setting up a schedule of reading each lesson, completing the assignment, and then critiquing your successes and deficiencies. Even though we are continuously self-critiquing our progress, this schedule provides you with a structure and perhaps a limited timeframe that will improve your progress. Of course, you can be flexible regarding time with these lessons, but you may see more growth with a schedule.

Here is a basic outline of the objectives for each lesson:

Lesson One: Learn what you have.

Lesson Two: Edit for two favorite themes.

Lesson Three: Photograph new images for one of those two themes.

Lesson Four: Begin learning the process of building a theme from past and new images (making new work is always encouraged in each lesson).

Lessons Five & Six: Practice what you've learned so far to build skill.

Lesson Seven: Discover ideas and resources for sharing your portfolios.

Lesson Eight: Complete and realize your photographic vision and passion.

Another approach to the assessment process after completing each assignment would be to enlist a fellow photo friend or a pro you respect to help you judge each assignment. You could share your work on Zoom or via another sharing method to get feedback.

By either method, you can take the feedback and apply what you've learned to the next lesson. You may see an issue with image quality, or discover a theme direction you hadn't keyed in on before that informs your next effort.

REPETITION: You may begin to notice that there is some repetition in the exercises we will complete throughout this book/ workshop. This is deliberate—true growth comes from practice, so many exercises need to be repeated as you continue to refine your images and your portfolio.

HOW TO VISUALIZE A PORTFOLIO USING LIGHTROOM OR OTHER SOFTWARE

I use Adobe Lightroom to access my photographic library and for some of my image processing. A major asset in Lightroom is the Collection module, which I use extensively to organize my photographs. I have dozens of collections and smart collections, some focused on specific projects, long-standing themes, and some based on ideas I have for future bodies of work. Some of those seedling ideas go nowhere, and some take root to form important bodies of work. Adobe Bridge has a similar Collections function. I also use Smart Collections to organize my images by rating, keyword, or chronologically by day, month, or year.

The curation process starts with downloading my digital files into Lightroom. Before I click on the Import button, I add keywords that are important for searching for specific photographs later on. As I edit, I rate them on both technical qualities and aesthetics. Both rating and keywording help me during each future editing session to be more efficient. I can go to a group of images in Folders or Collections and more easily pick up where I left off.

NOTE: In the context of this book, the words *edit* and *editing* refer to the process of refining a selection of photographs, not the post-processing of a single image. I will also use the words *curate* or *curation* to mean the selection, organization, and presentation of a collection of images.

When I am working in Lightroom, I often think of what Collection a photograph might fit in. In both my editing and field sessions, the theme ideas help funnel photos into my Collections. Each new photo session often has a few images that will build depth for that theme.

This workshop does focus on curation, but I also give you direction on how to build up depth in your portfolio themes. The process can take a short time, like my Antarctica portfolio, which was created in five days of intensive shooting. Or it can take decades, like my Yosemite portfolio that was created over forty-five years of living in or near the park.

I am working on a new Yosemite book, going through the same process of editing I describe in this book, narrowing my collection down to a strong set of images. I will be striving for the strongest balance of images that illustrate my decades-long love affair with Yosemite. Factors such as season, scale, lighting, and subject matter will all be considered. The images that are the most expressive and unique will receive the highest priority.

In each lesson, I will show you some of my editing process as I narrow down toward my final selection. These illustrations will give you a real-life example that should help you develop your own portfolio ideas. As with all of the examples shown in this book, you see my selections and can read about my thinking through that process.

The true value here is the time and effort that you commit to developing your portfolio.

For my Yosemite book, which I use as a personal example of portfolio development throughout this book, I want to assess my selection of waterfall photographs shown in the screenshot on the next page. They will be an important aspect of the overall book, so I turn to Lightroom's Survey Mode to get a clearer sense of what I have to work with. I can see if I have images that are too similar, and what styles of capture—like fast or slow shutter speeds—work together or don't. In terms of this book project, the waterfalls won't be sequenced together, but if you flip through the pages and notice the same waterfall again, that won't convey the range of waterfall images I have. In the lower-right corner of the second screenshot on page 4, I've included the same image in both black-and-white and color to see which one fits best in the overall grouping. Once you learn the value of the Survey Mode, you can use it often when you need to evaluate any set of images.

Beyond just waterfalls, I'll look for a balance of seasonal imagery, as well as a balance of scale, such as broad scenics versus smaller details of the landscape. I see how I like the balance of black-and-white versus color. These assessments are an ongoing loop, where my last Lightroom session will lead me to consider other photos, and reject some images that don't fit the group or don't match the quality of others.

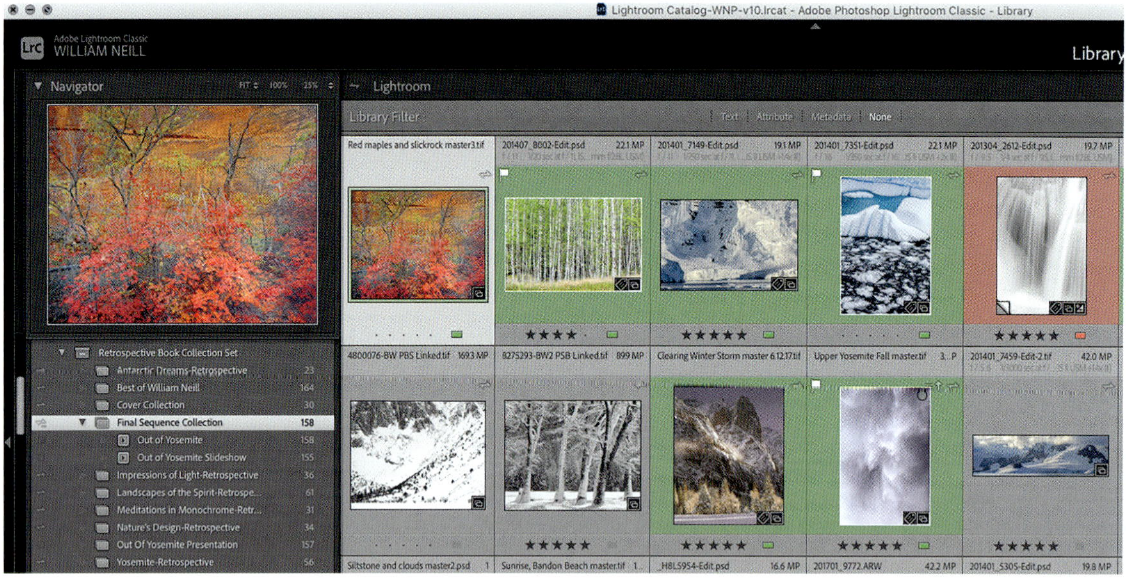

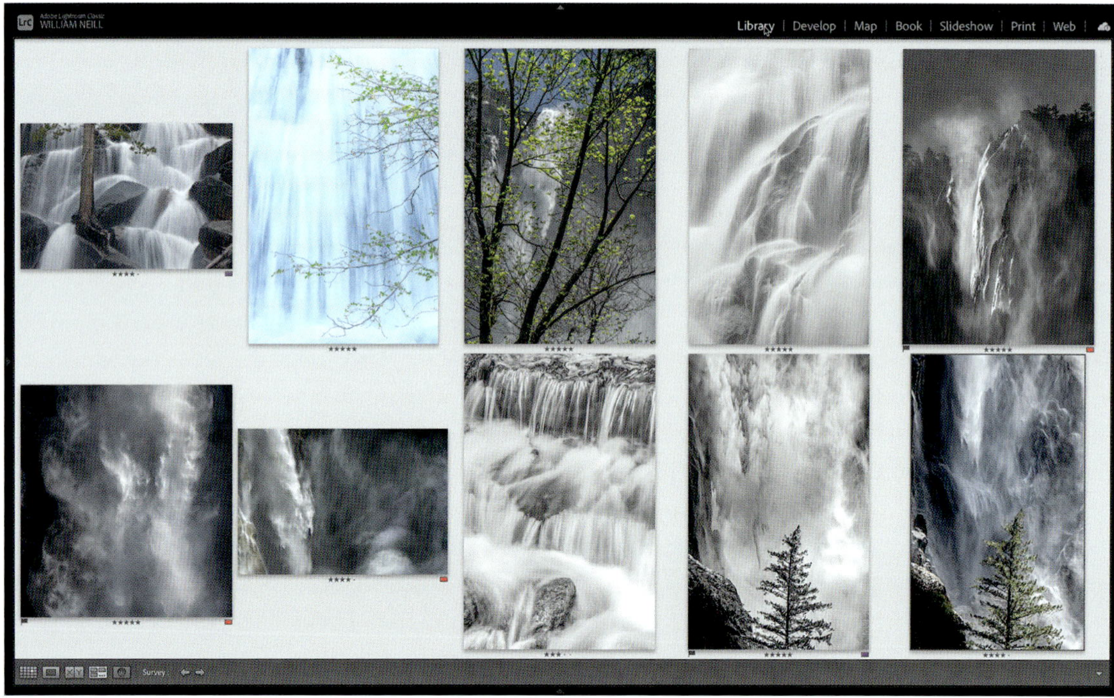

To make the most out of this book, I suggest that you create a Collection Set in Lightroom to organize your work as you progress through each lesson. Say you call that Collection "Portfolio Development." Then make a new Collection, nested inside the Portfolio Development Collection Set, for each lesson. As you browse through your image library for a given lesson, make it the Target Collection so you can tag your selects, sending them into the lesson folder.

Although I prefer to use Lightroom, you do not need it to work through this book. You can use your preferred image-processing software or organization system, and organize your photos by lesson.

Let's get started!

At the back of the book (pages 101–106) you will find a resource that includes lesson summaries as well as a worksheet to help you work through each assignment. This resource is also available as a downloadable PDF at: rockynook.com/portfolioworkshop

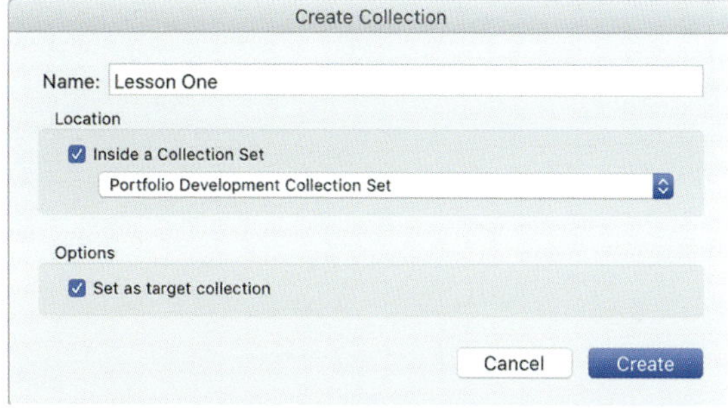

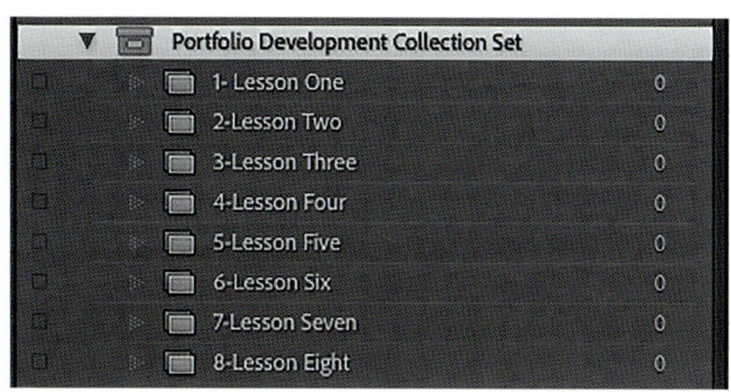

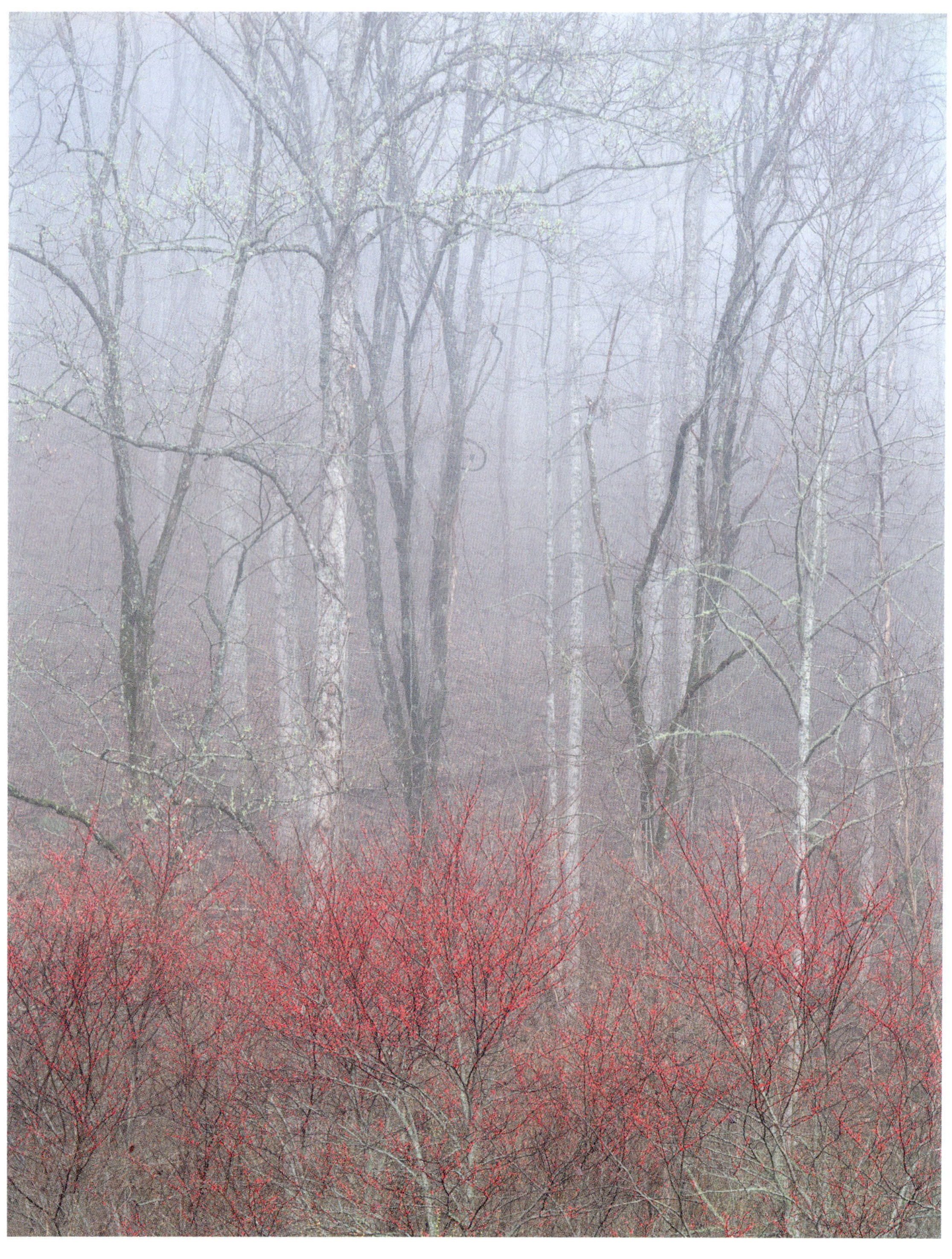

Redbud in Fog, Great Smoky Mountains National Park, North Carolina, 1991

FIND YOUR FOCUS!

OVERVIEW

The objective of Lesson One is to begin to understand how to develop a cohesive portfolio that reflects your vision.

ASSIGNMENT

Identify twenty to thirty images that you believe are among your best and that comprise your favorite themes. (The assignment is described in more detail on pages 14–15.)

What kind of photographs do you make? The most common answer I hear when I ask this question is: "Oh, I try a little of this, and a little of that." Throughout the workshops I have taught over the years, the seductive power of the camera is clear in student work. Since the visual explorer is naturally pulled toward many subjects, the class portfolios I review most often indicate diverse interests but little focus.

The world is full of wonders to photograph, but how many of us have the time to take every branch in the road? The hectic pace of our lives, and the expediency of clicking the shutter, conspires to distract us.

WHY MAKE A PORTFOLIO?

Based on my experience as a professional photographer and teacher, I believe that many photographers would benefit from a more focused approach to their photography. If you see something of yourself mentioned above, consider what subject matter *really* inspires you. The subject can be broad or narrow, such as forests or maple trees, deserts or Death Valley. The important thing is to focus on a theme or two, and to photograph with the idea of creating a focused portfolio.

Creating a portfolio is a natural process for most of us who wish to document our lives and tell stories through our images. We make picture albums of family trips and special occasions. For serious photographers, organizing their most expressive photographs to create a web-page gallery, submit for an exhibit proposal, or present to a publisher is nearly essential to distinguish themselves from the others in their field.

WHAT IS A PORTFOLIO?

Let me take a minute to give you my definition of a portfolio. I consider a portfolio to be any body of photographs that has a consistent theme and is of consistent quality. The theme can be as broad as "my photographs"—the theme being defined by the fact that you took them! This broad definition is often impractical in that the range of images has meaning only to the photographer and a few close friends or family members.

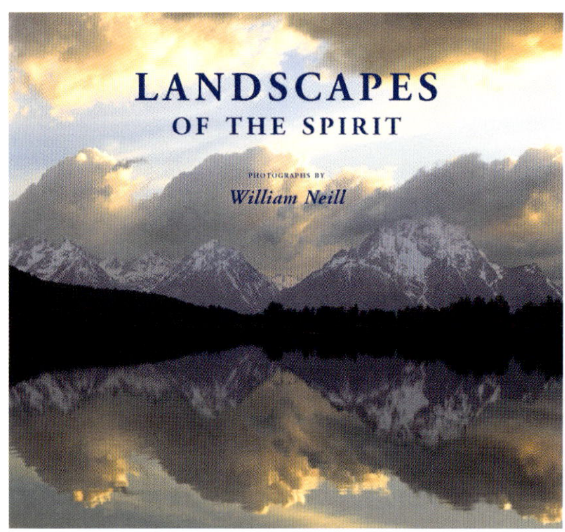

There must be a coherent theme that moves you and motivates you.

I find that, most often, it is best to show a focused and consistent body of work for marketing or presentations (such as to show fellow workshop students or a local camera club). For example, my book *Landscapes of the Spirit* contains my favorite and most spiritual landscape images.

Your portfolio can take many forms, including the following:

- An actual portfolio box of fine prints
- A book
- An online presentation or web page
- An exhibit of photographic prints

The idea is to make photographs and then curate them to put your best images on the subject in one place.

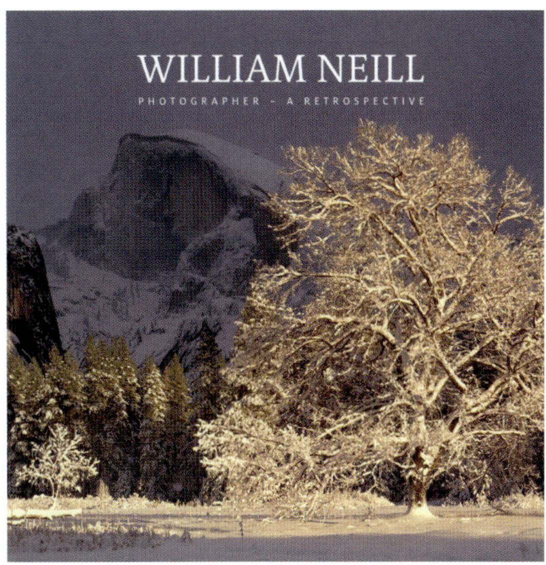

I recently learned how valuable building themes has been for me. When I approached a publisher about doing a book together, I told them of my previously published books and about my thematic portfolios from which I had created a small series of eBooks. They came back to me with an offer to do a retrospective book, and I quickly said yes. I already had the chapters planned out, most of which I developed over a few decades: Landscapes of the Spirit (my main theme), Yosemite, Impressions of Light, Meditations in Monochrome, and By Nature's Design. My Antarctic Dreams portfolio was photographed in five days, but I felt the body of images held up to my standards.

BEGINNING THE PROCESS: PORTFOLIO PREREQUISITES

There are two main requirements for your portfolio. First, there must be a coherent theme that moves you and motivates you. Let's say that you have picked a theme of landscapes with some aspect

of water involved. Possible images could include waterfalls, rivers, lakes, or the ocean. The focus of your photographs doesn't have to be objects or places, but can also include actions, such as water flow, or a style of capture, like my *Impressions of Light* series in which I use intentional camera motion. You could also organize images by your processing style, like I did with my high-key *Whispers of Light* portfolio.

The second criterion is that there should be *no one image* that is of lesser quality than another. In any situation where you show your work, great images can be diluted by the average images you might use to "fill out" your presentation, and the overall impression of your photography is reduced. These decisions are subjective, which makes it difficult to know who to listen to. Showing your photos to peers and pros you respect is a good start.

Ultimately, you are the artist and therefore need to develop the ability to self-assess your work. Listening to others is part of that, but as you learn to trust your *own* instincts, you will gain self-confidence. Confidence gives you freedom to explore creative directions. There are no failures, but rather only lessons learned. Many aspiring photographers do not give the editing process enough priority.

BUILD YOUR PORTFOLIO

The next step is to go through your files to find the very best images of your chosen subject, be it waterfalls, portraits, flowers, or lighthouses. If you adhere to my second premise—that no one image should be of lesser quality than another—you will find the elimination process difficult. Being self-critical is critical! Don't be surprised if you find only a few images that are of equally high quality for a given new theme. The ultimate editor is

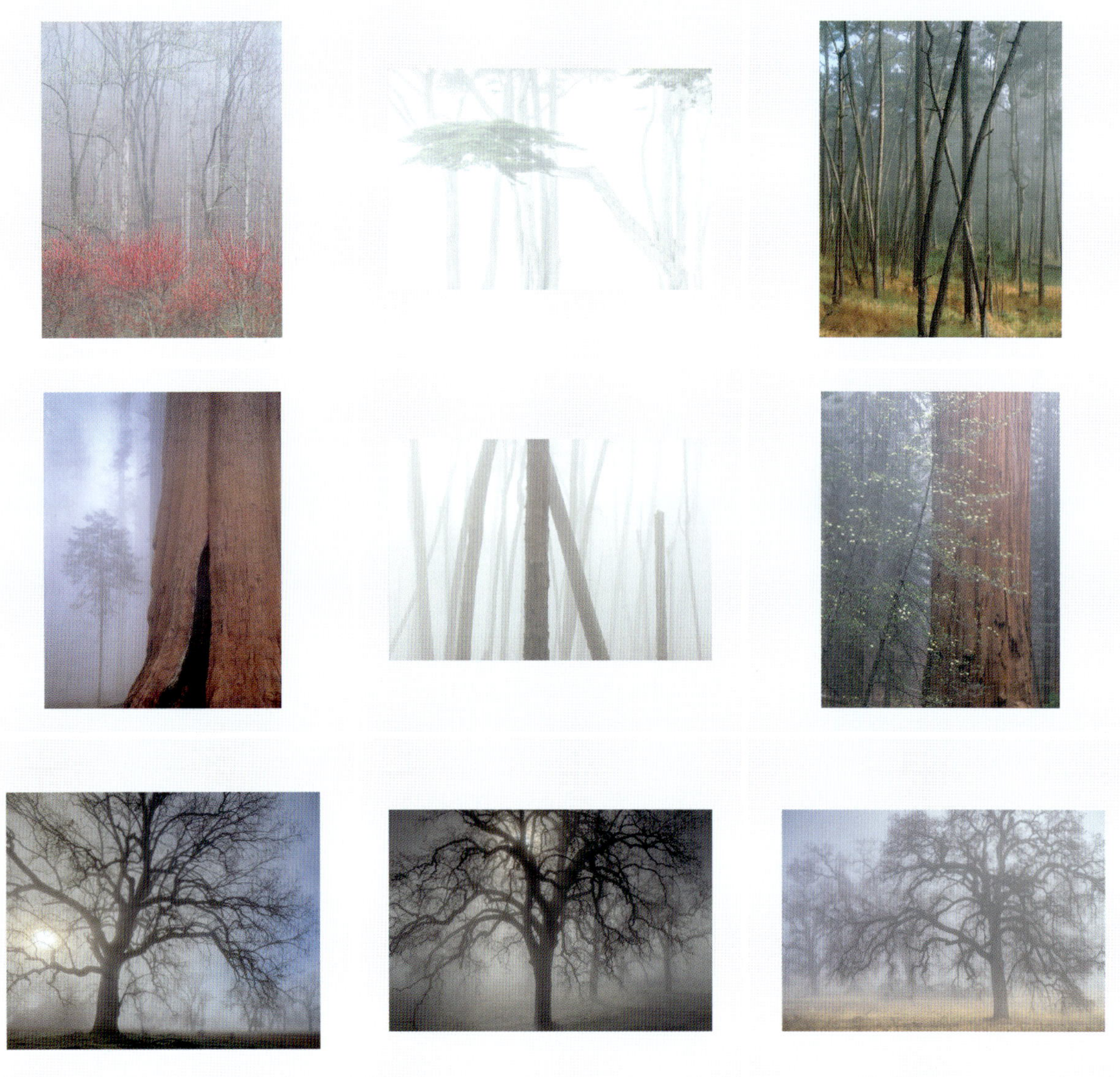

Here is a small portfolio of tree photographs that I feel are coherent and consistent in quality, style, and theme. I will call it "Forest Fog." Titling a portfolio will make you think hard about exactly what you want to say and help direct the viewer toward your interests, your theme. When I use the Survey module in Lightroom, I can see what variety I have on that subject or see if I have too many similar frames. In this example, I feel good about the image quality. I look at the bottom three frames and wonder if they are too similar, or if they expand or magnify the visual impact of "trees in fog." For me, it depends on the context—for example, whether the photos appear together on a book spread, or are fading one into another in a slide show presentation. I will talk more about "context editing" in Lesson Five.

you, the artist, but you may find it valuable to have your work evaluated by another, more experienced photographer. This "second opinion" approach will either confirm your assessment or force you to reconsider the level of your imagery.

FOUNDATION FOR GROWTH

Once you have completed your initial selection, you have created the foundation for your portfolio, be it two or twenty images. This selection becomes your baseline from which to measure your progress. When you continue to photograph for the portfolio, your planning, exploring, image-making, and editing will be concentrated on that theme. New images are compared to your highest quality standard and can be added to the portfolio *if* they measure up. Over time, new photos might replace the original images as the portfolio's overall quality is elevated. The photographs that endure, the ones that still excite you, remain in the portfolio. By evaluating this collection of premier images often, you can see and are rewarded by your progress. Even if you don't share your portfolio, the process serves as an excellent tool for self-evaluation.

Being self-critical is critical!

Making photographs for a particular portfolio could last for just a few months or for a lifetime. Like many nature photographers, I love to photograph trees, and I have an ongoing tree portfolio. Many years ago, my images were chosen for a book project to illustrate novelist John Fowles's essay entitled *The Tree* (The Nature Company, 1994). The book provided an opportunity for my images to complement a classic piece of environmental writing with a strong message about the human need for wilderness.

Here is a photograph of mine, *Trees Growing on Moss-Covered Boulders, Baxter State Park, Maine, 1995*, that has assumed a high position among my select tree photographs. As is often the case for me, creating this image began with discovery and a sense of wonder. The roots of these trees thoroughly amazed me with their grace and determination! My judgment of the image rests on the overall technical quality, that I feel the image is as good as my best tree photographs, and that the image reconnects me with the sublime experience of being there.

GOALS FOR THIS BOOK

Once you have explored a theme in depth, and hopefully you have seen your own vision of the subject grow and coalesce, you will probably find other themes in your work to cultivate into new portfolios. Creative thinking along these lines may lead you to themes that evolve from your own personal passions and that are yet unexplored by other photographers. The potential for rewards in terms of personal satisfaction, the refinement of your presentations, and gaining attention for your work are increased. The first level of creativity comes with the image-making, but the next phase comes with the editing and organization of images in ways that reflect your unique style and perspective.

Find your passion, develop depth, edit tightly! Simply put: Focus!

NOTE: If you haven't read the Introduction, please go back and do so before moving on, as it explains the structure of this book and how to approach the assignments. You'll also see reference to a worksheet at the back of the book that will help you as you work through each assignment.

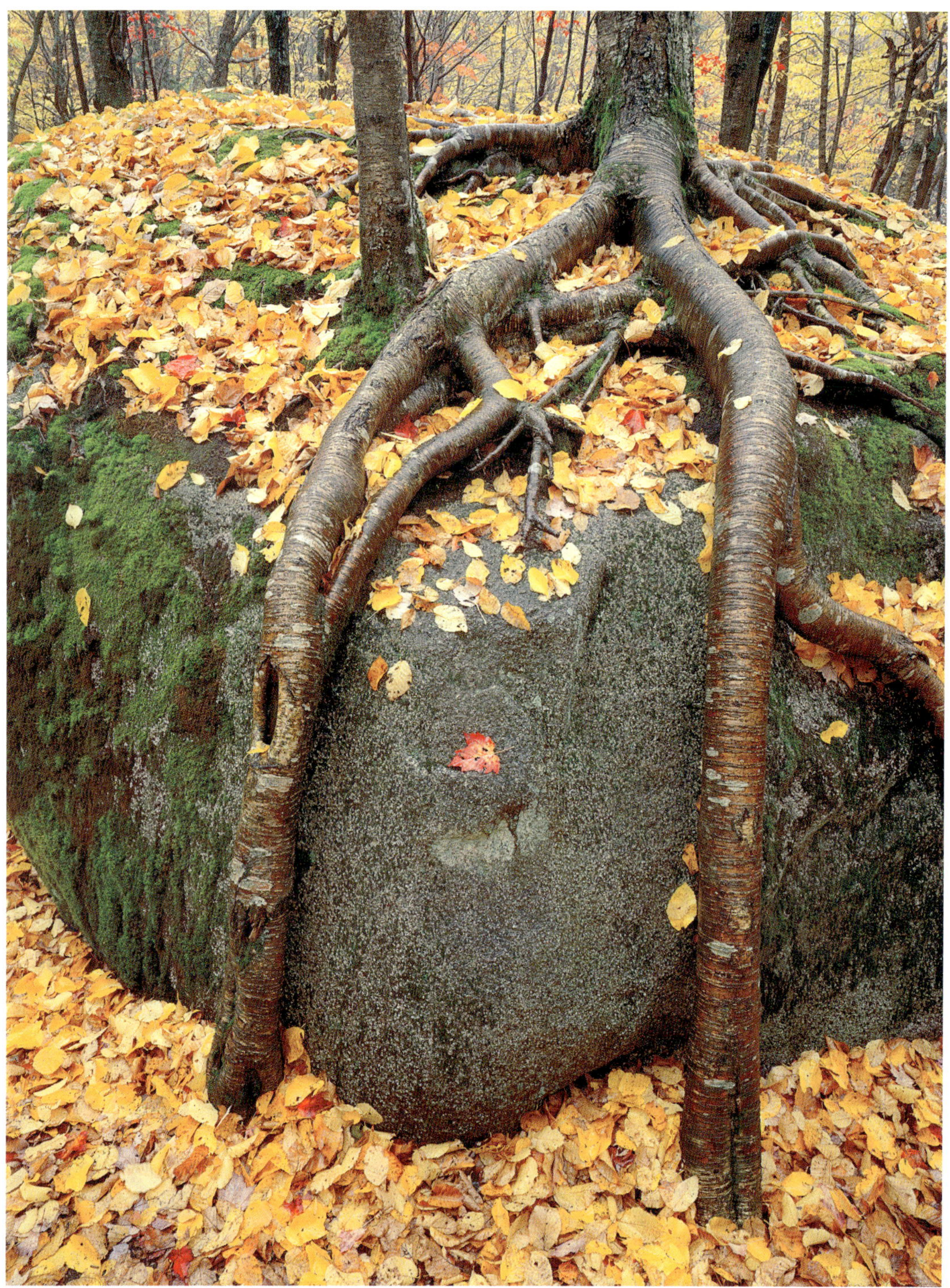

Trees Growing on Moss-Covered Boulders, Baxter State Park, Maine, 1995

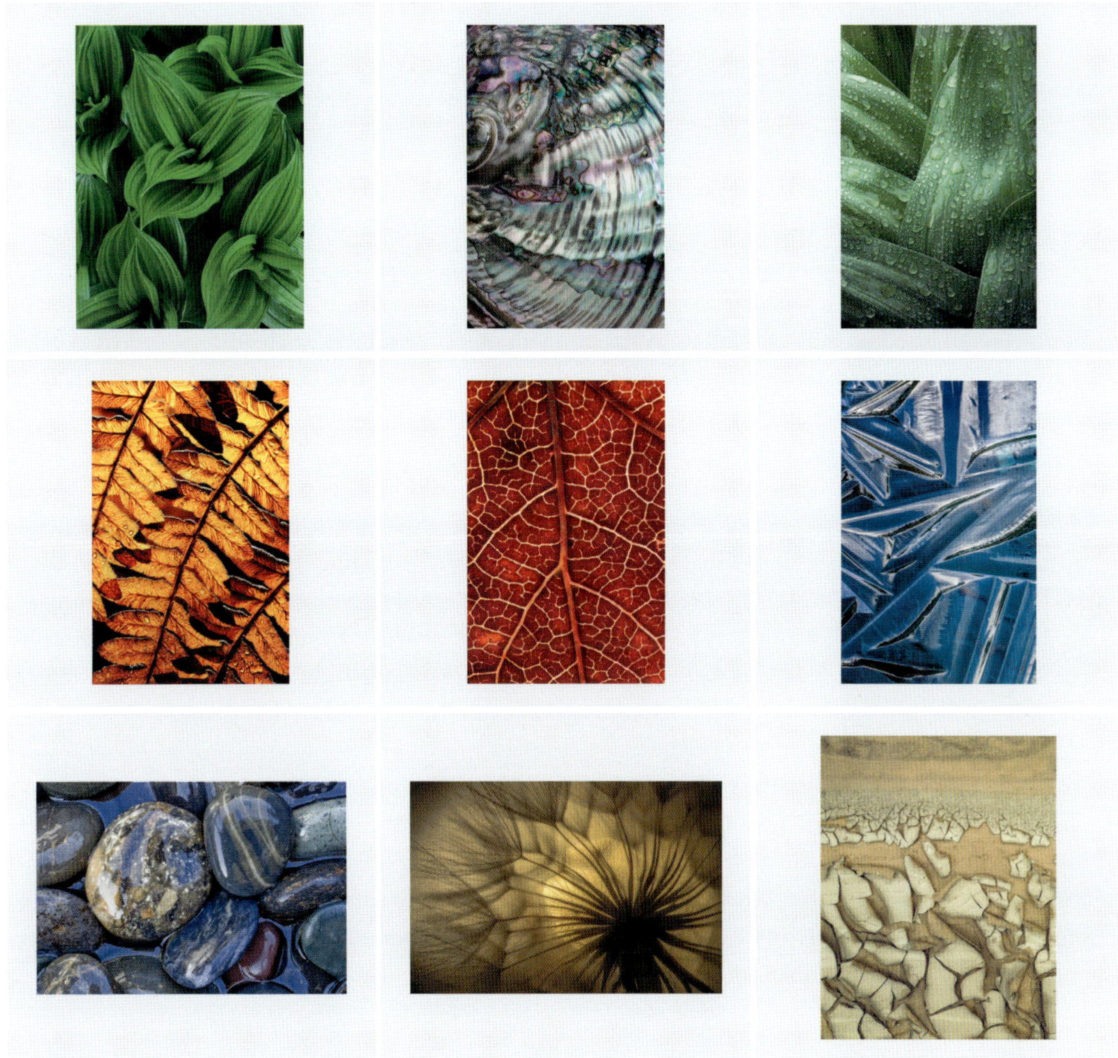

Here is a small portfolio I call "By Nature's Design," which is also the title of a book of mine. I think it is a cohesive group in regard to the images' strong graphic design and colors. Each pattern is different and the quality is consistent to me. I also feel that this example illustrates a less literal and more creative direction for a theme. The original book was a science-education project to define and illustrate how the patterns we see work as described by the publisher: "Underlying the many modifications and adaptations of patterns that occur in nature is a hidden unity. Nature invariably seeks to accomplish the most with the least—the tightest fit, the shortest path, the least energy expended."

I was attracted to and photographed patterns in nature before working on this book, and then I built upon that library of photos to illustrate the author's writings. The book is long out of print, but my enthusiasm for nature's designs has not waned. My example here shows photographs I created over the course of forty years, with the most recent being taken just a couple of years ago.

YOUR ASSIGNMENT: FIND YOUR FOCUS

This first assignment is largely an assessment process. Create a new Collection in Lightroom (or whatever software you use to organize your images), then place some of your favorite and most expressive work in that folder. I suggest you start with 50–100 photos, then narrow the selection down to a minimum of 20 images and a maximum of 30 images. As you choose your images for this assignment, start looking for subjects or themes that reoccur often in your photography. A theme can be literal, based on a place, such as India, or on an object or subject, such as dogwood trees or waterfalls. But your concept could be metaphorical, such as a selection of flowing water images that, through a title like Flowing, stand for freedom or moving forward through life.

In our next lesson, you will begin to work more specifically with these themes, and in future lessons you will make new images to add to your selected themes. Therefore, it is important to look for themes focused on subject matter that will be accessible during the time period you've allotted to work through this book, especially considering the season or travel restrictions. If at all possible, find a subject that you can photograph at home—inside, outside, or around your neighborhood. If your theme is related to autumn, and it is actually autumn, then that is the right time. If it is wildflowers and it is not spring or summer, it will be tough to make new images within that theme!

As mentioned above, during the course of this book, we will work toward adding new images to your portfolio. For this assignment, however, I want you to concentrate on past work. I want you to learn what level your work is at, what quality level you've achieved. It doesn't matter what that level is because it's all relative. We all want to improve. Learning to curate your work and learning to organize it into portfolios is an excellent way to monitor your progress. Consider both the technical and emotional qualities of your images when you sort through your work. Try to judge each photograph's merits relative to the other selections.

I usually start this process in Lightroom by doing an initial review of my photo session, checking my exposures, composition, and sharpness. The creative potential of each image is always on my mind as I make my technical analysis, so much so that I often jump into the Develop module to play with the sliders or tweak the cropping. As I go through the set, I make initial ratings, starting with a low number that I increase if the photo gets elevated later on.

As my editing continues, I often find a few similar images that I need to compare. For example, I might need to judge which photo is the sharpest if subject motion was an issue, such as in images with wind blowing leaves on a tree. The Compare function in Lightroom is indispensable for this kind of comparison. Let's say I'm judging a group of ten similar compositions: I'll start with the Survey tool so I can see all ten frames, clicking the Tab key to simplify the selection. After I get that group down to the best few, I then switch to the Compare mode.

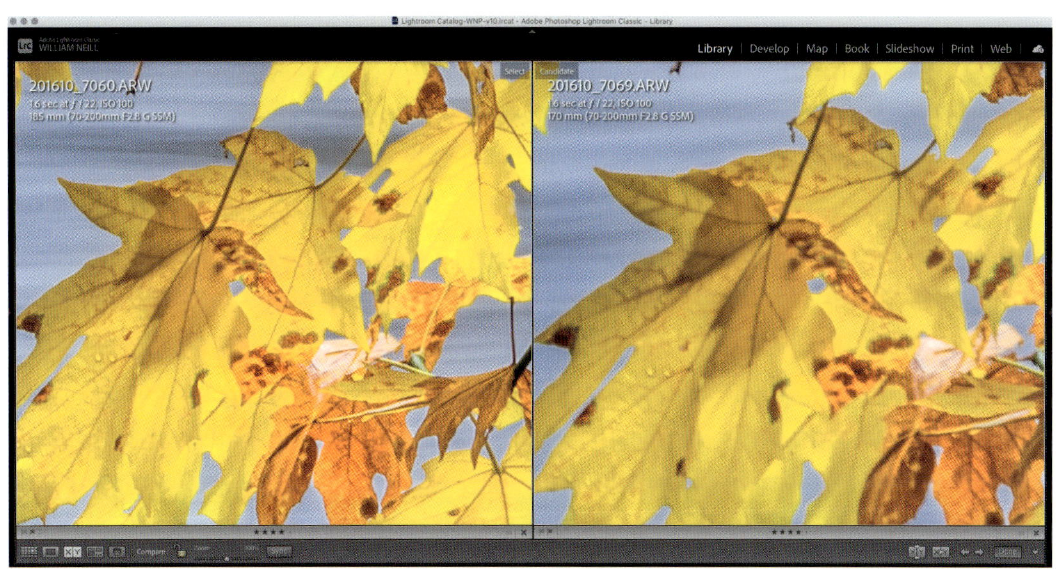

Compare Mode in Adobe Lightroom

When I teach my portfolio development course, I tend to see photographers struggle with three main issues when they are reviewing their work and selecting images for a collection. First, I often see a wide range of subjects within each collection. But this is okay, as the overview gained from this assignment is vital as we go forward. Second, I often see inconsistent image quality in the selection. This is okay, too, because once you narrow down the theme direction, it is much easier see your strengths and weaknesses as you survey the collection. Third, I often see that adding keywords and rating images have not been given enough attention. Without keywords, it is much harder to find all the available images for building a particular theme. And without ratings, the act of narrowing down your selection is harder because you must keep going back into past photo sessions to find the best images.

REMINDER: Sticking to just one or two themes will be very helpful as you advance through the lessons in this book. If you jump around trying out too many themes, you will not see the full benefits of a focused development of a theme or two.

NOTE: When you first look at your selection for Lesson One, I suggest using Lightroom's Survey mode. Think about possible directions for your themes. When you put together this first selection, make your own assessment of the quality and concept. Then move on to Lesson Two and do the assignment based on your assessment.

YOSEMITE PORTFOLIO CASE STUDY

Throughout the lessons in this book, I will use a Yosemite book project that I'm currently developing to help illustrate my selection process for you. To get started, I created a Collection folder to gather any images that I might consider including in the book. As with the assignment I have given for Lesson One, this initial grouping contains many more images than will be used in the final project. I know that the book will contain anywhere from 100–150 photographs. I made the Collection a few months ago and I keep adding to it when, in the course of my normal work in Lightroom, I come across a good candidate for the book.

Since these selected images are coming from the Library module, they already have post-processing applied, as well as ratings. I know that eventually I will be narrowing down the number of images.

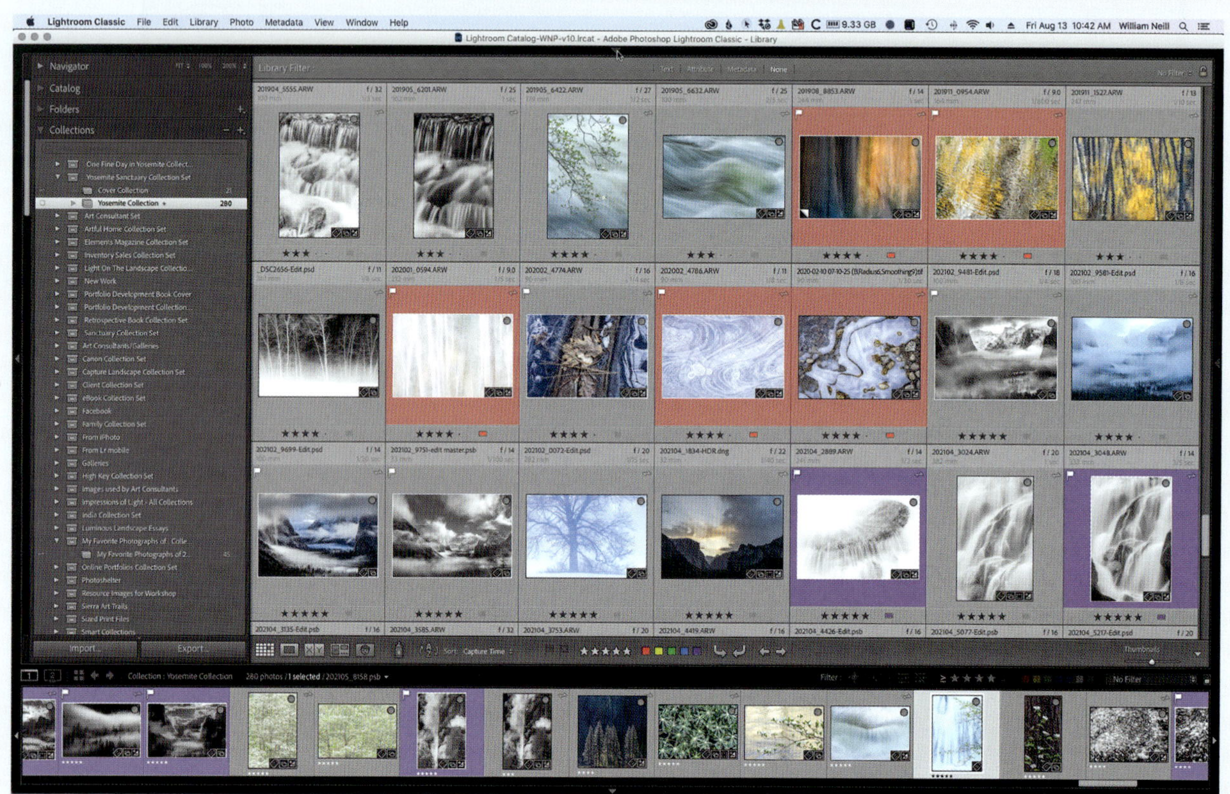

My default rating system is to use stars, and all the images I bring into my Yosemite Collection will have a high star rating. When I get further along with narrowing my selection, I will add a notation such as flags or color. One approach I've used is to give the "definitely in" photos one color mark, like green for go, while the "maybes" get another color, like a yellow flag for proceed with caution. I don't set a rule, as I have many images being marked and sorted for many possible projects at a time and I'll often change a photo's color mark when I move from one project to another.

In these examples you will see a broad range of images that I am considering. I've included some similar photos about which I am uncertain in this early stage when one does not need to be too critical. The screenshots show my early initial selection, much as if I were submitting the selection for my own assignment.

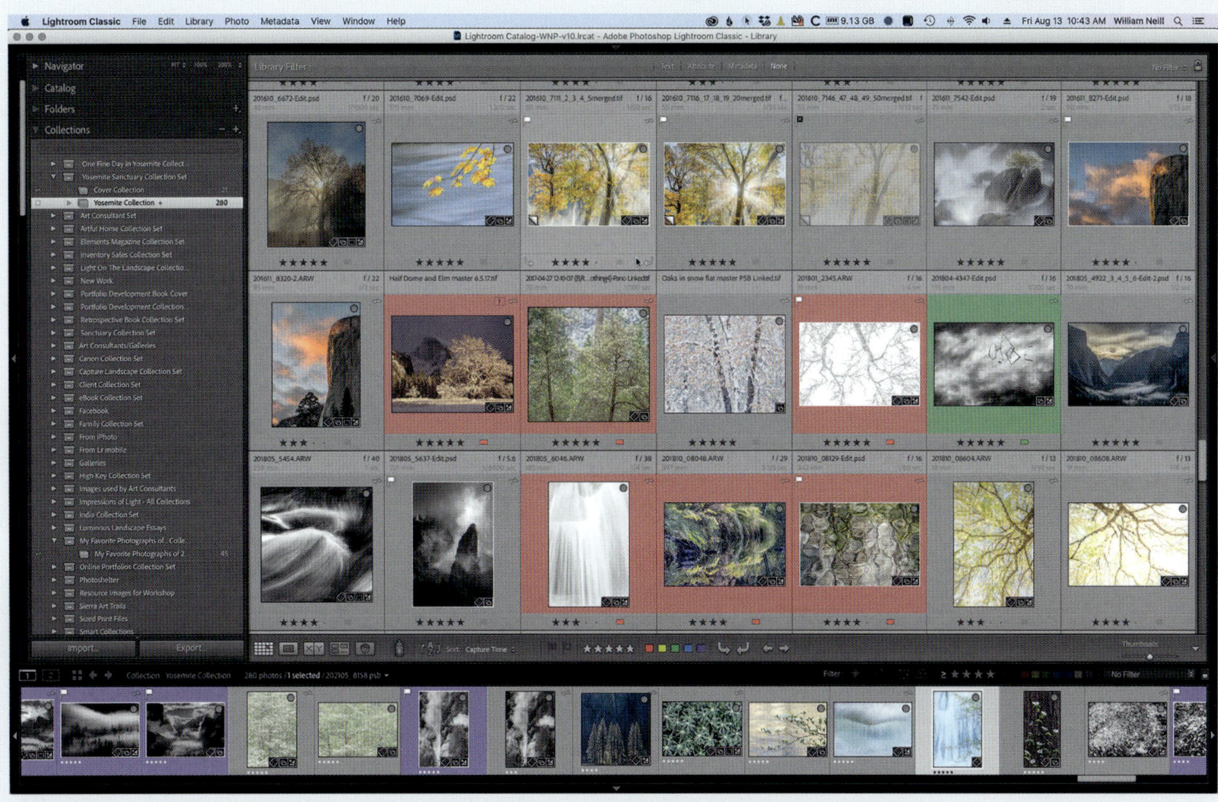

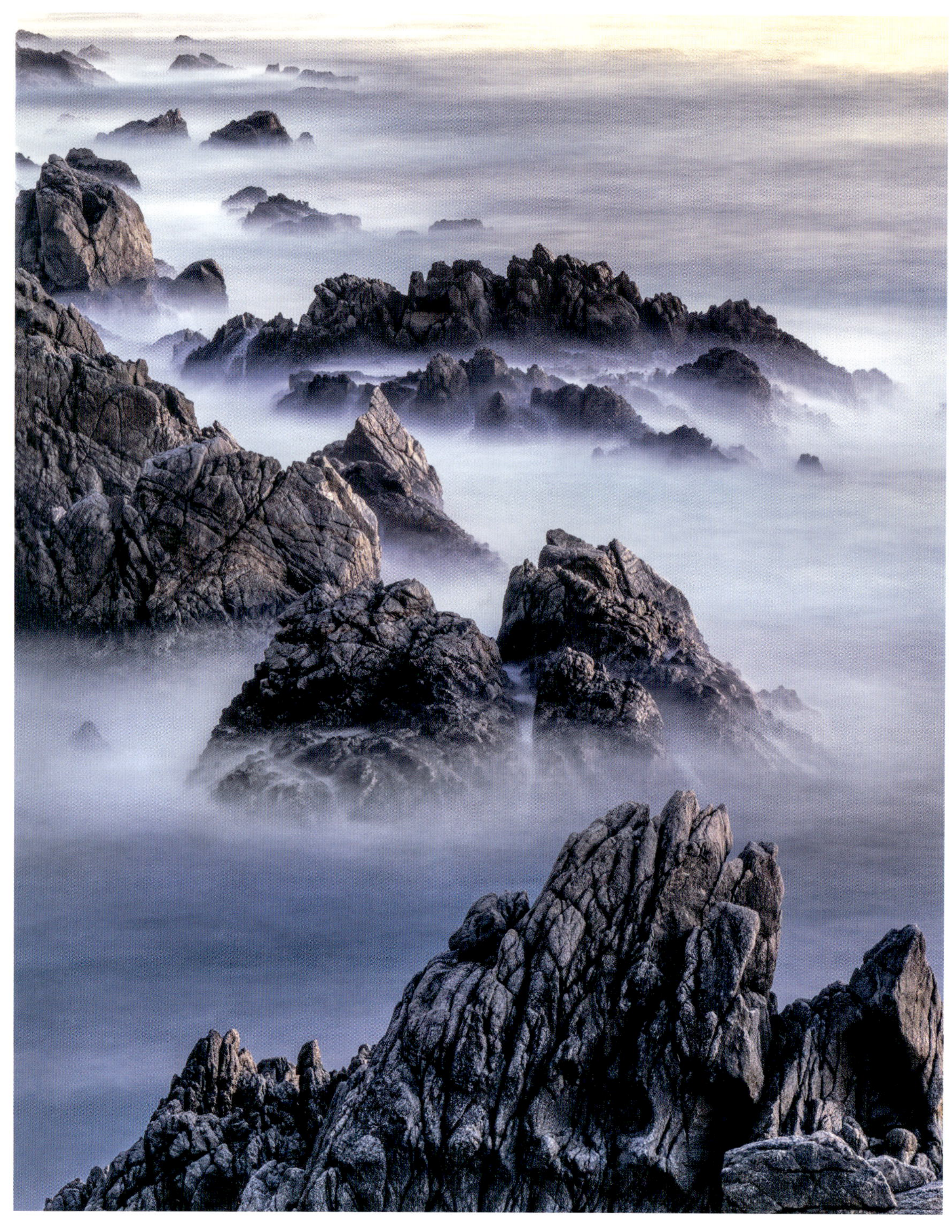

Twilight, Big Sur Coast, California, 1995

THINK IN THEMES

OVERVIEW

The objective of Lesson Two is to begin to organize your photographs by theme. This first step in the process will help you find your strongest themes. Then, once they are established, you will refine and build upon the themes with existing images from your image library.

ASSIGNMENT

Pick two themes about which you feel passionate and that show off your personal vision. Choose up to ten images that represent each theme (for a maximum of twenty images total). Being highly selective is key. (The assignment is described in more detail on page 24.)

The photographer's task is to explore, photograph, and share with others the multitude of exciting aspects of our world and our lives. We show others what and how we see—that which they might otherwise miss. What a joyful job!

Our busy lives make it challenging to find time to photograph the subjects about which we are most passionate. Many amateurs are just happy to get out to photograph on the weekend. Many pros are distracted by the demands of running their business, from filling orders to marketing to keeping current with the latest technologies to managing employees. I include myself in this second group!

FINDING THEMES

Throughout the lessons in this book, I want to help you concentrate your attention on developing thematic portfolios so you can determine which images are strongest and weed out the lesser images. The first phase is to see what themes exist in your photographs, then analyze which photos are the most promising and start editing those images into a portfolio that exemplifies your best work.

PULLING THE WEEDS!

In the past, when I would work with students in a one-on-one workshop critique, I often found a few good images mixed in with many lesser ones. The overall impression was not as good as it could have been. When I pulled out the weaker images and set aside the best ones to define a more effective portfolio, the photographer instantly became better! Even when setting aside only two or three "best" images, good editing elevated the photographer's sense of achievement and ability. It clarified for me, or any viewer, of what the photographer was capable. It is this positive experience that I hope to duplicate in this book.

EDITING EVOLUTION

It is important to remember that the curation of a collection of images is an ongoing process. As you begin to assess the current level of your work, you also learn to maintain that standard of quality through your editing skills, and you become conscious of ways to improve your future efforts. There is no scientific way to do this, so we must rely on our own instincts and observations and the opinions of others. Our instincts depend on how well we feel an image translates our vision and the subjective process of comparing our photographs to others.

It is important to remember that the curation of a collection of images is an ongoing process.

In the early years of struggling to launch my career, I remember saying to myself, "my images are that good," when looking at other photographers' published work in magazines or books or calendars. At that early stage of one's development, it's hard to know if, in the outside world of judgment, our own assessment is realistic or not. The judgment of editors, curators, art directors, teachers, and publishers was especially critical when I came up since there was no social media or Internet on which to share images so easily.

Ideally, many of us want to make photographs that we are pleased with, and we aren't too worried about others' thoughts. Still, it is enjoyable to have our images appreciated by others beyond family and friends. If you are interested in developing a reputation as an artist, you'll need to build up your editing skills. Unavoidably, we end up comparing our work to others. If done in moderation, judging your images against others can provide healthy motivation and confidence like I experienced as a young man. If overdone, comparing yourself to other photographers can easily lead to discouragement and frustration. Proceed with caution!

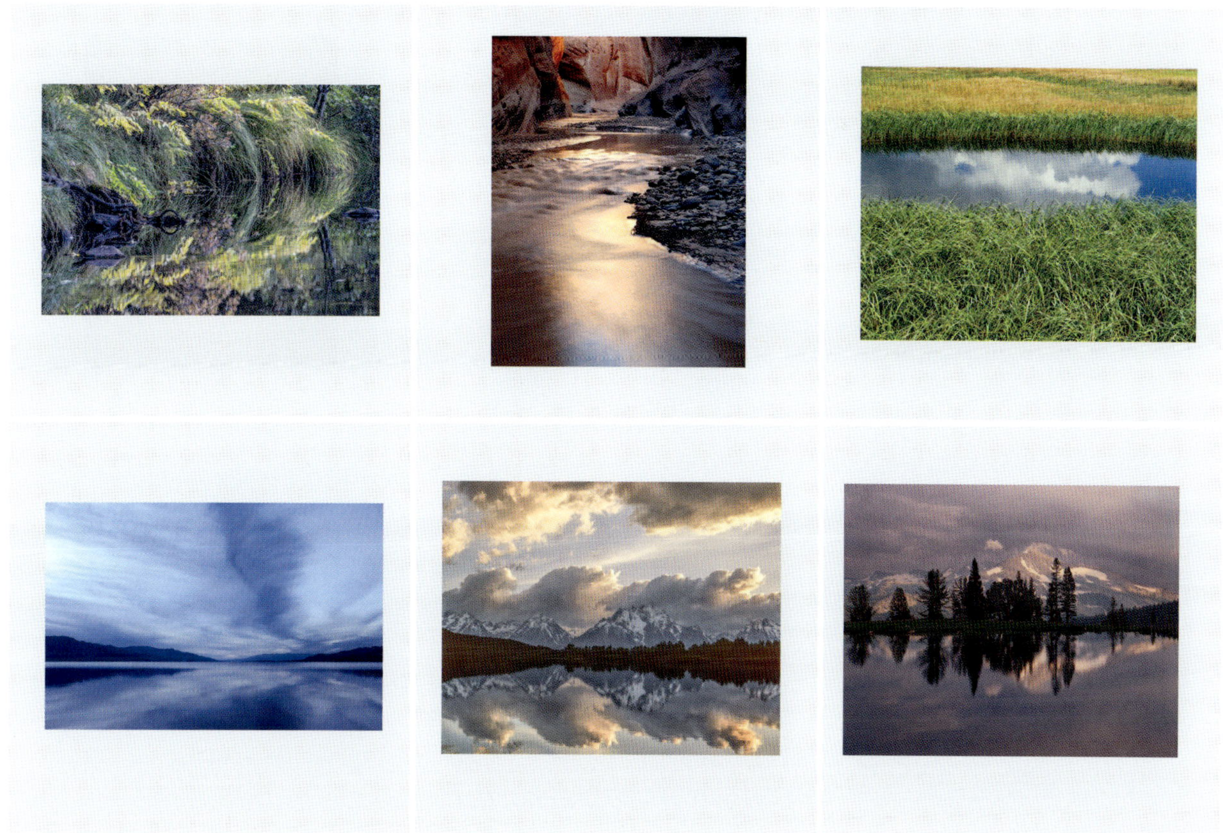

I'll use these six images to illustrate different options for finding themes in your work. Hopefully, how I think about organizing my photographs will give you some ideas about curating your own. These six photographs are organized into a group entitled "Reflections." They work okay as a group, but something is not quite right.

The bottom three images from the group are a bit too similar for such a small grouping. If the portfolio has at least ten or more photos, their similarities might not be so evident. If I take one of the bottom three out, and don't place the remaining two adjacent to one another, the balance of the five (shown on the next page) works better.

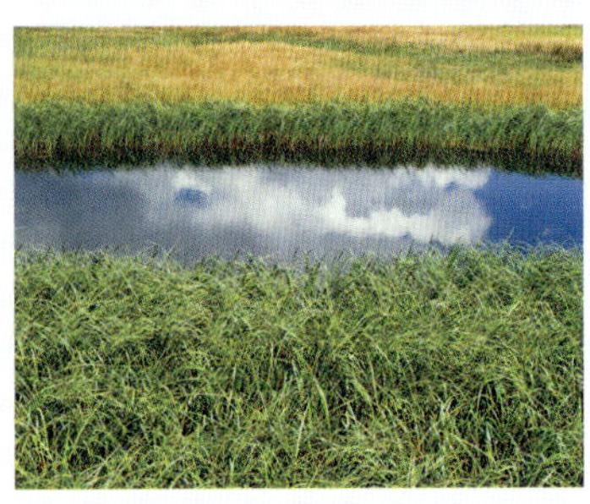 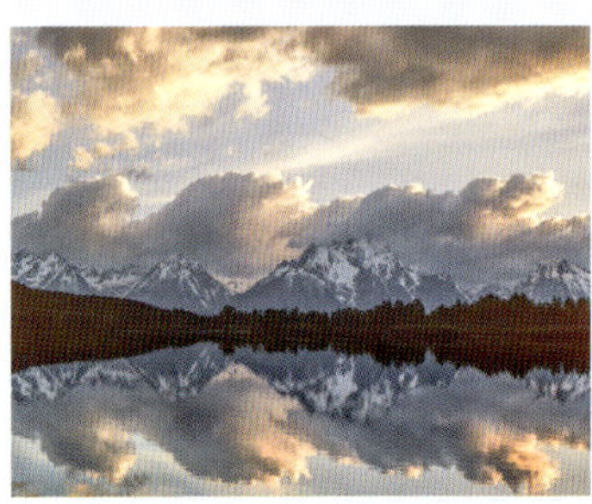 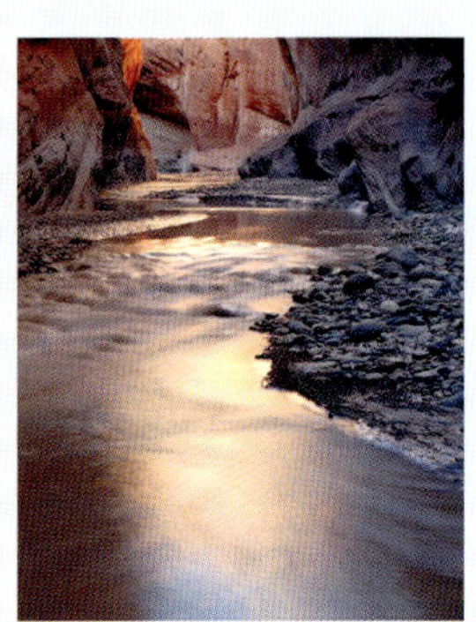

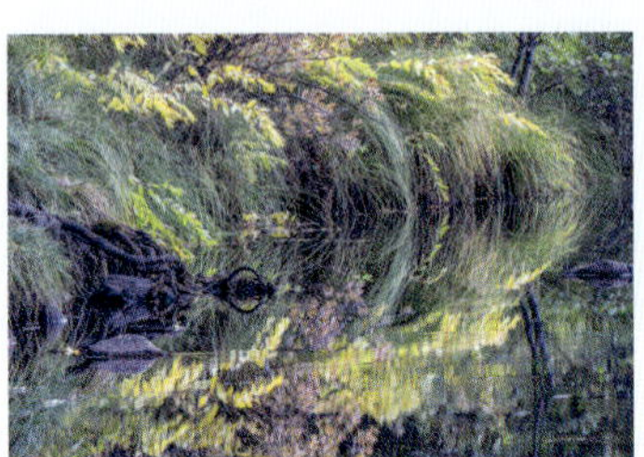 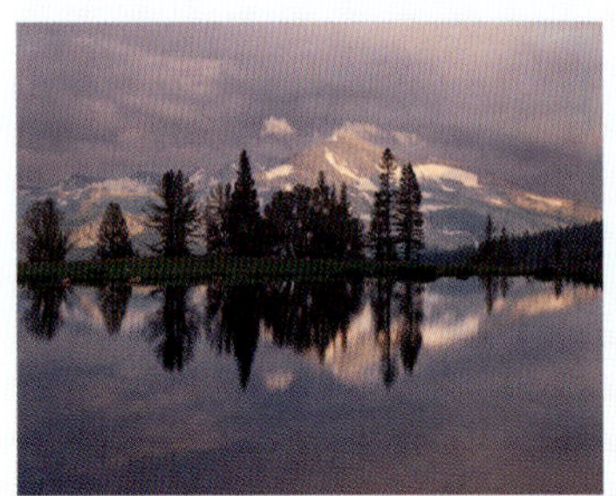 

The balance of these five images looks better to me, and I eliminated the sense of repetition I had in the first group simply by removing one "symmetrical" photo and shuffling the order.

The bottom three images from the first grid might also point the way to a new direction, that of "Symmetrical Reflections."

The top two corner images above—*Cloud Reflections and Grass, Yosemite* and *Reflections, Paria River, Utah*—fit the overall "Reflection" theme. Yet, I find them fitting into another reflection theme where only the reflection itself is included, without its source. I may find that I have more images (of equal quality, of course!) that fit this theme, or this may lead me to find more photographic opportunities for this new idea while out photographing. It may lead me to go where I might find more "Just Reflections" images.

These are exercises in tightening up a theme to create a balanced group by refining the visual themes. I could also take the group of five in another direction, by expanding my "Reflections" grouping into a "Water" portfolio.

When I can see all my "Water" images together, I notice that I have five surf images out of the eight. Two others are ripple reflections. My analysis is that I need other types of water images such as waterfalls, river rapids, or lakes. I see my tendency to use slower shutter speeds is repeated in most of these images, so I would look for some water images that use fast shutter speeds and show strong textures in order to break up the pattern of blurred water images (unless, of course, long blurs are part of the theme idea).

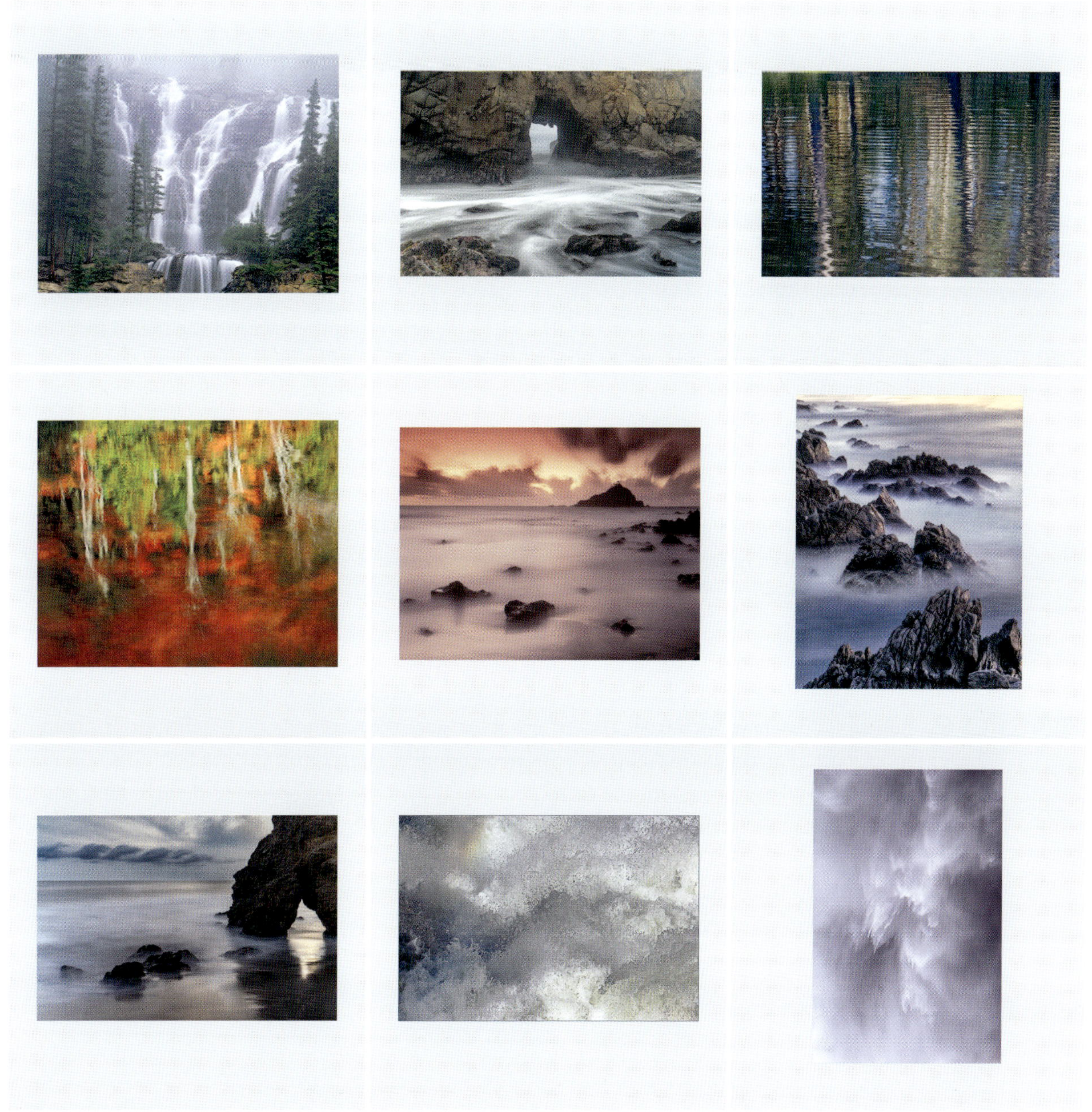

On the opposite page is a small collection of portraits from Rajasthan, India. I wanted the group to show both the faces and colorful dress of these women. As I browsed through my library and then organized the images into a "Portraits" collection, I noticed that I mostly preferred the frames that show direct eye contact. So, in the grouping here, I would remove the bottom-left photo to make the "eye to eye" aspect more strongly apparent.

YOUR ASSIGNMENT: CHOOSE THEMES

Pick two themes about which you feel passionate and that show off your personal point of view, and that include images you feel are unique to you. As mentioned, it will be helpful to pick a theme that allows you to add images as you work through this book, especially considering the season.

When you begin looking through your images, consider both their technical and emotional qualities. Try to judge each photograph's merits relative to the other selections within the theme so that the collective group is of equal, or near equal, quality.

In following lessons, we will work toward adding new images to your existing portfolios. For this assignment, however, I want you to concentrate on organizing your images into strong themes. Dig deep to make sure you find your best work on your chosen subjects! You may include images from Lesson One if you wish. Hopefully, you have made note of your own thoughts about Lesson One, and any feedback from others will give you some ideas on what themes to pursue as you work your way through this book.

I suggest that you select ten images each for your two chosen themes, for a maximum total of twenty images. Once you finalize the selection for the two groups, take a break. Come back to review them a few hours or a day later with fresh eyes. If possible, share the selections with a mentor or photo peer for feedback. For me, taking a break helps tremendously, often clarifying the best direction in terms of quality and my passion for the theme. Specifically for the progression of these lessons, you will want to pick out the theme best suited to the time period you may schedule for the eight lessons.

NOTE: Before selecting images for Lesson Two, look at your submission for Lesson One and analyze your photographs and possible directions for your themes. Then move on to Lesson Two and do the assignment based on your assessment.

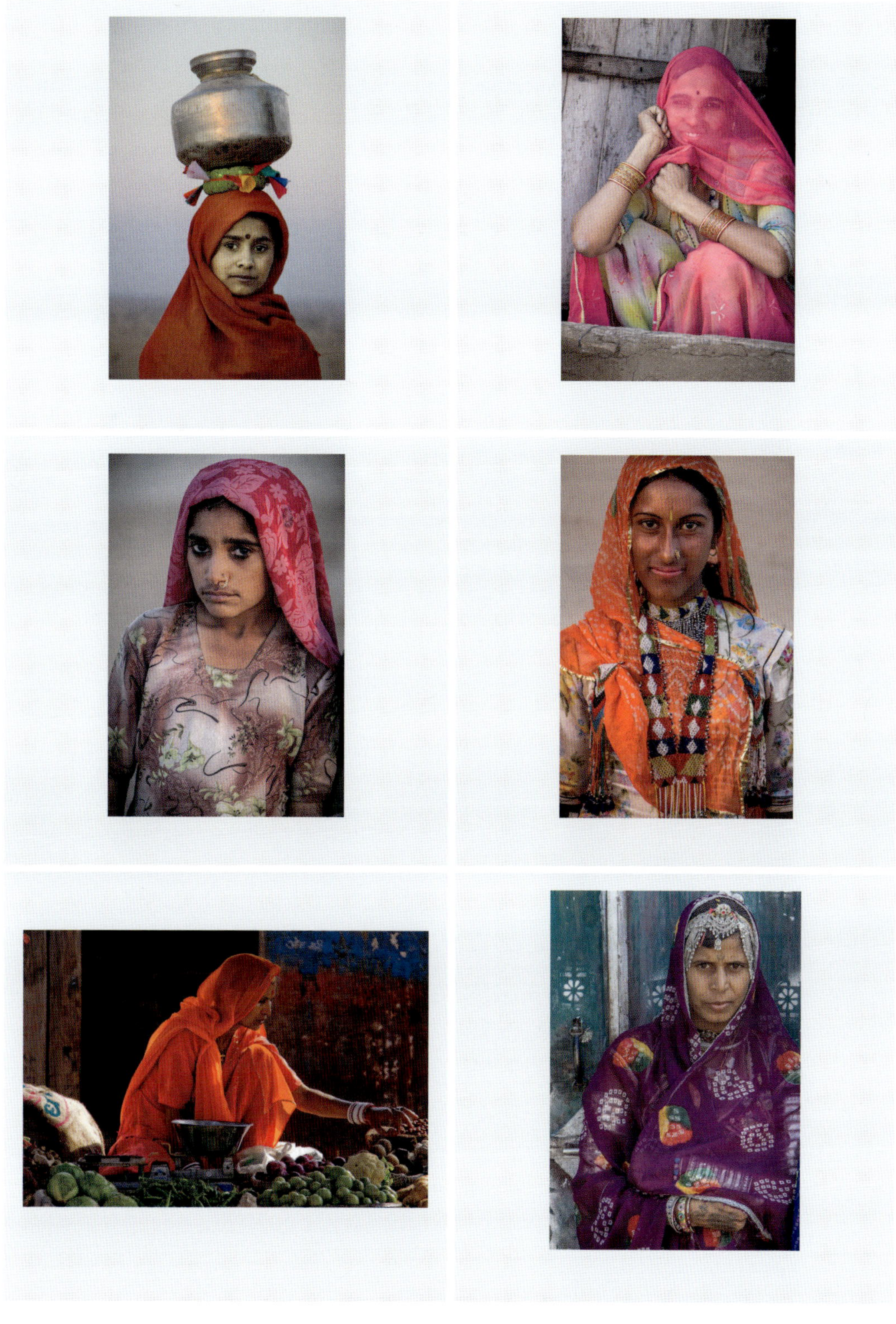

YOSEMITE PORTFOLIO CASE STUDY

One aspect of the selection process for my Yosemite book is that I wish to include work made in the broader Yosemite ecosystem. The regions of the Sierra Nevada surrounding the park's border have been important for me in my development as an artist. I lived in the Merced River Canyon just west of the park for twenty years. The eastern slope of the mountains to the east—which include Mono Lake and the canyons that run east out of the high peaks of Yosemite—are important to the ecosystem and have been a haven for me photographically. In the grid below, I have picked ten photographs and assembled them in a collection I call "Beyond Yosemite."

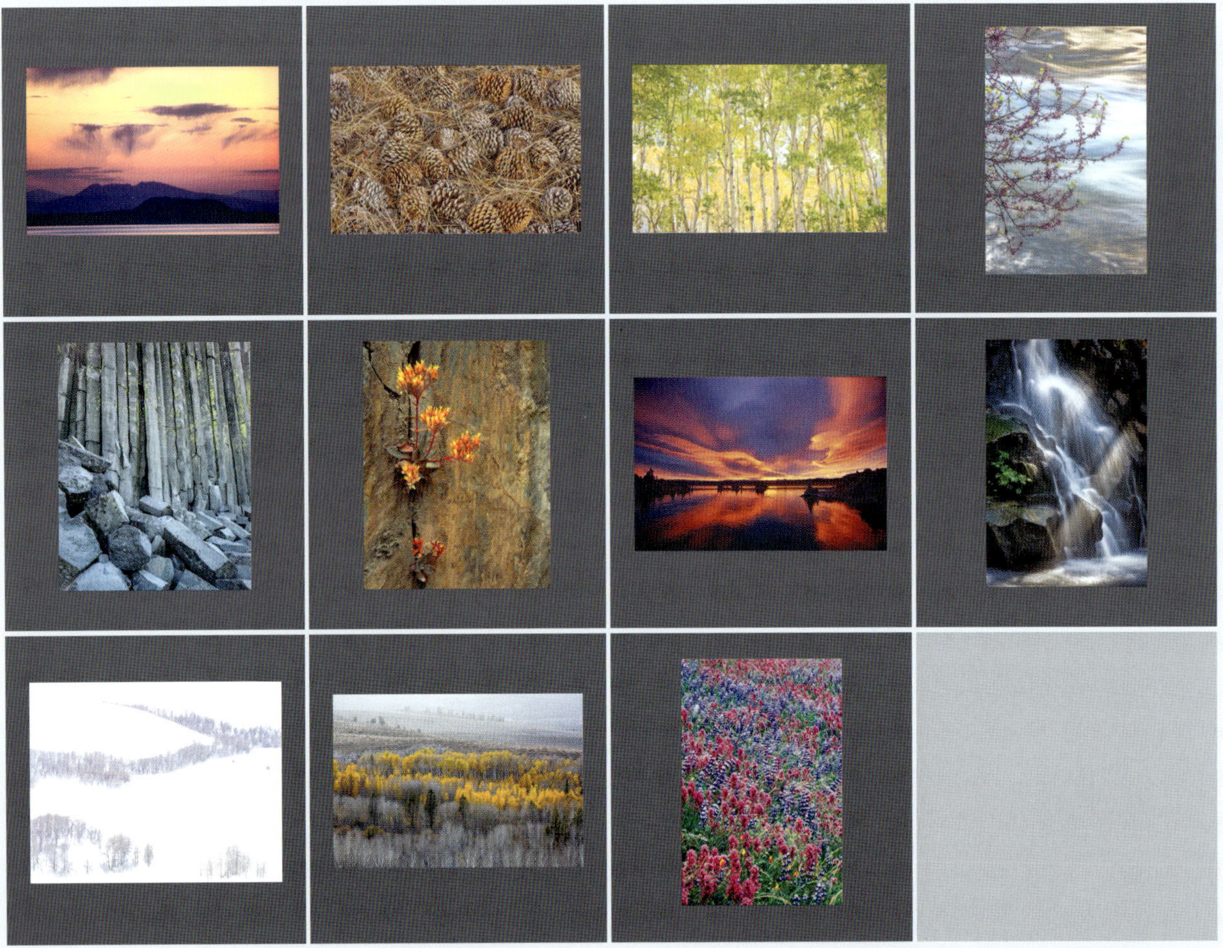

Another critical aspect of my Yosemite work is the close-up details that I always seek out when I explore the park. My grouping below is my theoretical submission for this assignment; I picked these from my broader collection for the book. I chose close-up photos showing a variety of color, seasons, and subject matter. Although, if selected, these photographs will be dispersed throughout the book, this group allows me to judge where my process stands, and what might be added to improve my selection for the final book.

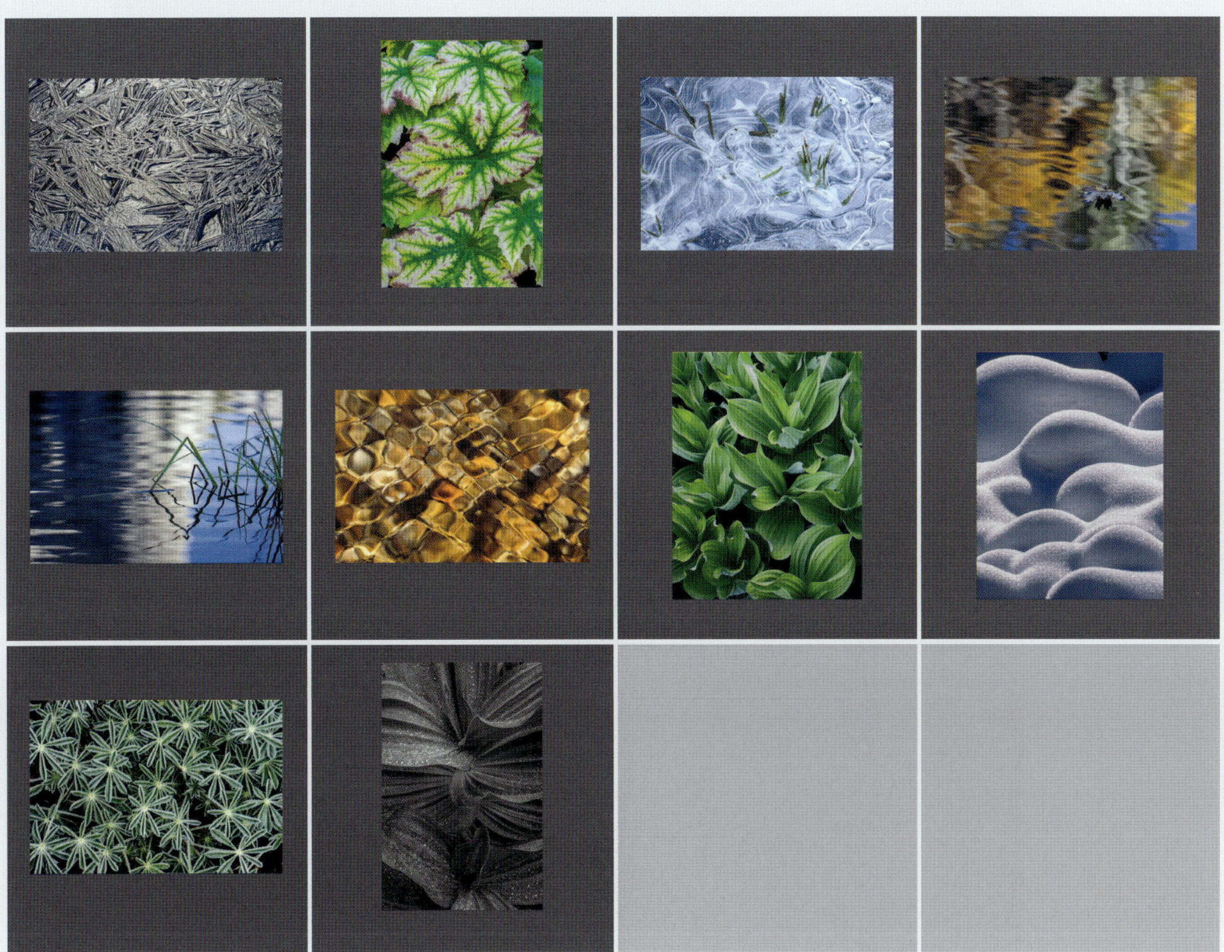

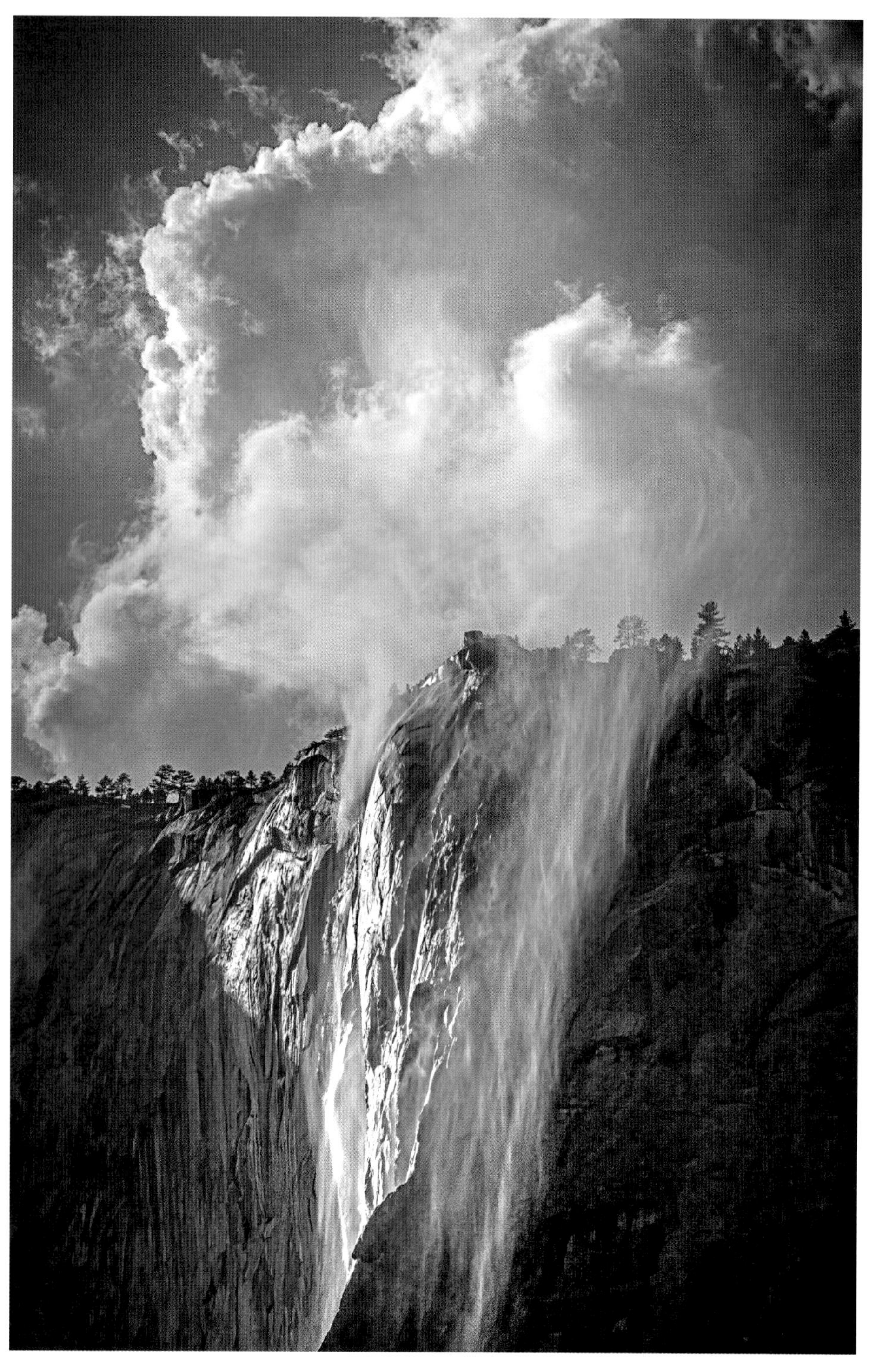

Horsetail Fall and Storm Clouds, Yosemite National Park, California, 2019

EDIT ON A TECHNICAL AND AESTHETIC LEVEL

OVERVIEW

The objective of Lesson Three is to photograph for a specific theme of your choosing.

ASSIGNMENT

Make all new images (not previously exposed photos) with a clear theme in mind, then analyze those images using both technical and aesthetic criteria. (The assignment is described in more detail on page 34.)

It is useful to have a visual sense of what creative photographs look like. We all know that feeling—while browsing through a magazine, book, or website—of seeing an image that takes your breath away. The image probably has great light, or a captivating graphic design, or an unforeseen perspective, or all of the above. The techniques applied—that of exposure, the placement of objects within the frame, etc.—are faultless and invisible in those magic images. Whatever the technical qualities we might ascribe to the image, most importantly there is a sense of freshness, of innovation. If we stop to think about our reaction to such a photograph, we realize we have just been shown the world in a new way. We sense a creative effort before our eyes. Naturally, this effect is what we want in our own images.

VISUAL LITERACY

Learning to see creativity in photographs, in our own images or in those created by others, is a difficult, subjective, and ongoing process that involves developing what is called *visual literacy*. Visual literacy in photography can be defined as the understanding of basic elements of visual design, technique, and aesthetic qualities of an image. It is a knowledge or memory of images seen, and the understanding of what makes images succeed or fail.

Skill in visual literacy includes the ability to apply what we have seen to our own work. It is like knowing the history of a photographic subject. We all have looked at thousands of images. It is this history stored in our brains—the memory of our favorite photographs made by our favorite photographers; those seen in magazines, books, or calendars; those of our own successes and failures—that forms our visual literacy and that influences our own compositions.

LET HISTORY BE YOUR GUIDE

We must remember the famous quote, "Those who cannot remember the past are condemned to repeat it." I am a landscape photographer and have found that my study of well-known landscape photographers and their photographs has provided me with a library of imagery that I use as a reference. This reference works for me when I am standing behind the camera as well as when I am editing. If I set up my camera in front of Half Dome in Yosemite (I have lived in the Yosemite area for forty-five years) and try some compositions, my mind subconsciously references my library, my memory of Half Dome images, and I tend to skip over compositions that seem too familiar.

One way to improve your visual literacy is to research images made of your chosen topic. If you are concentrating on flowers, then look through any related books or magazines you have, research online, or visit your local library to begin to see how other photographers have approached photographing flowers. I prefer to look at the work of established fine art photographers, rather than images that might be too generic. I look for the most innovative approaches to a genre for my inspiration, such as those that might be found in a museum or a large-format coffee-table book.

Some photographers have adopted an approach to discovering their unique way of seeing that is almost exactly the opposite of mine. Called *photographic celibacy*, this idea is based on the belief that many of us are too easily influenced by other photographers and photographs. The method is to not look at other photographers' work to avoid copying their style, locations, and so on. I completely understand and respect this theory, but to me one of the joys of life is to see the world through the eyes of other artists. I trust my instincts enough to be influenced and inspired by another's work but not imitate them. I would also trust my editing eye to recognize this issue in my work and be able to focus in on my most unique work and avoid redundancy. If you don't know what photographs have already been made, how do you know you haven't duplicated another's efforts?

I was fortunate enough to have known Ansel Adams before he passed away in 1984, and I learned from him the importance of being true to one's personal vision. I believe that every person has a unique perspective, and the first step to realizing that potential is to believe this is true, that it applies to you!

SETTING YOUR STANDARD

It is also important to establish a personal standard of quality for your portfolios. Defining your goals will help in this process. For many avid amateurs, their goal is to improve to the point where they gain recognition for their images, whether that means selling, winning contests, exhibiting, or publishing their photographs. For others, they just want to have fun with their photography. Their goals are more modest and less competitive, and so their standards are set at a comfortable level. They don't feel the need to push themselves. Either approach is fine, of course, as long as one's efforts are in line with one's expectations.

Our first two assignments have been ones of assessment, and after you've self-evaluated the selection, I hope you have a better sense of where your work stands. A standard of quality is relative, so don't worry about anyone else, just about improving yourself. If you know where you are, you can better see where you want to go, and you can judge when new images reach or exceed that standard.

Once a benchmark of quality is in place and some general goals are set, a feedback loop is established, giving you a way to monitor your progress: benchmark > new work > assessment > add successes to portfolio > reject lesser images > learn from successes and rejects. There will be an ebb and flow to the process; it's not always linear, but you will see progress.

The best way I know of to assess images is to lay them out and start sorting. If you have slides, use a lightbox. If you have prints, clear off a table or use the floor to spread out the selects. I use Lightroom Collections, as mentioned in the introduction of this book. I can easily set up thematic folders, move images in and out of those folders, and reorder the images within these "portfolio" folders.

LOOK FOR CONSISTENCY

In any circumstance when showing your work, the overall sense of consistent high quality will help your images become memorable to the viewer. It could be for a casual presentation to your local photo group, or if you are marketing your photographs, the proverbial first impression is very important. I once showed my best images to a book designer, and he remembered my images six years later, giving me my first book project!

EDITING ON A TECHNICAL LEVEL

Technical excellence is required for creative success. A camera is a tool for the photographer, just as a paintbrush is for a painter, and a hammer for a carpenter. Good compositions, exposure, choice of lens and camera position, and depth-of-focus control are all tools for creative image-making. I am going to assume that you have a basic understanding of photographic technique. If you feel lacking in this area, there are a multitude of books, workshop courses, and online tutorials that can help.

When you sort through your images, technical quality is usually the first point of decision. When looking closely at your work, either with a good photography loupe or when enlarged on a computer screen, you learn a great deal about your field technique. Make sure to look long enough to find out what you did wrong. We all tend to skip over our mistakes quickly. John Sexton, a well-known black-and-white photographer, once said, "The only difference between me and my students is that I have made more mistakes!" He means that he made more and learned a great deal from them. Learn from your mistakes, and then remove them from the selection process.

After I have assessed their technical quality, I think about which of my remaining images actually say something, something beyond, "Here it is," and "I was there." I look for magic and mystery. I look for an image that makes the ordinary extraordinary, or an extraordinary subject discovered and revealed.

Bottom line: Curate your images carefully. Learn from your mistakes. Take what you have learned, then go out and photograph some more!

Here are two waterfall images. I like one much better than the other. Can you guess which one? Which one do you prefer? Well, there is no correct answer to a question like this, except the photographer's personal choice relative to how the photograph might be used. Hanging on the wall in the living room? Entered into a fine art competition? Or if you are more concerned with commerce,

which one will sell better? Asking and answering these questions is called editing! We will talk more about selecting for context in upcoming lessons.

If you're curious, I prefer the image on the right, as it fits my aesthetic approach to composition, which tends toward minimalist, clean, and uncluttered design. The extra-long exposure adds an ethereal quality for me.

Here is another group of waterfall images. Let's say I am preparing for an exhibit featuring waterfall photographs in a prestigious gallery. My primary consideration is to share my best and most personal photographs. Location is not a consideration. I've X'd out the photos that I feel are compositions I've seen elsewhere and that are less distinctive of my personal style.

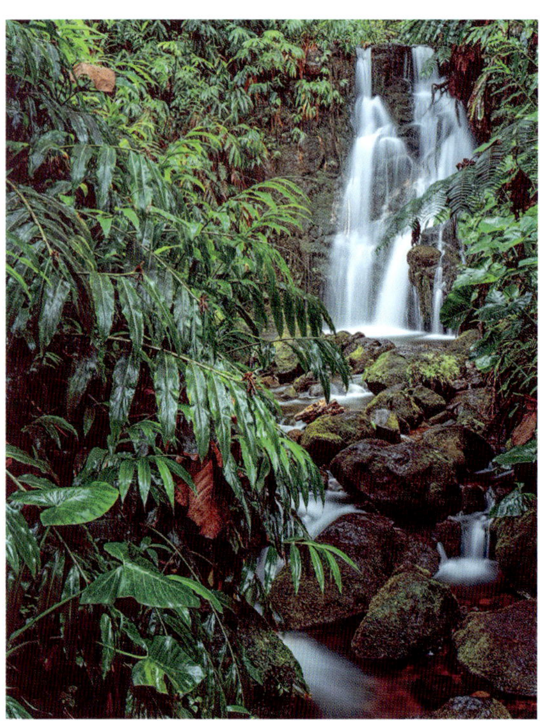

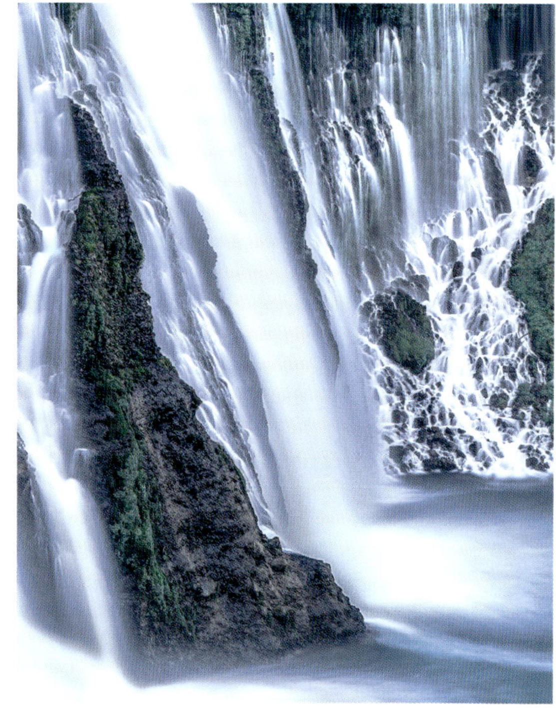

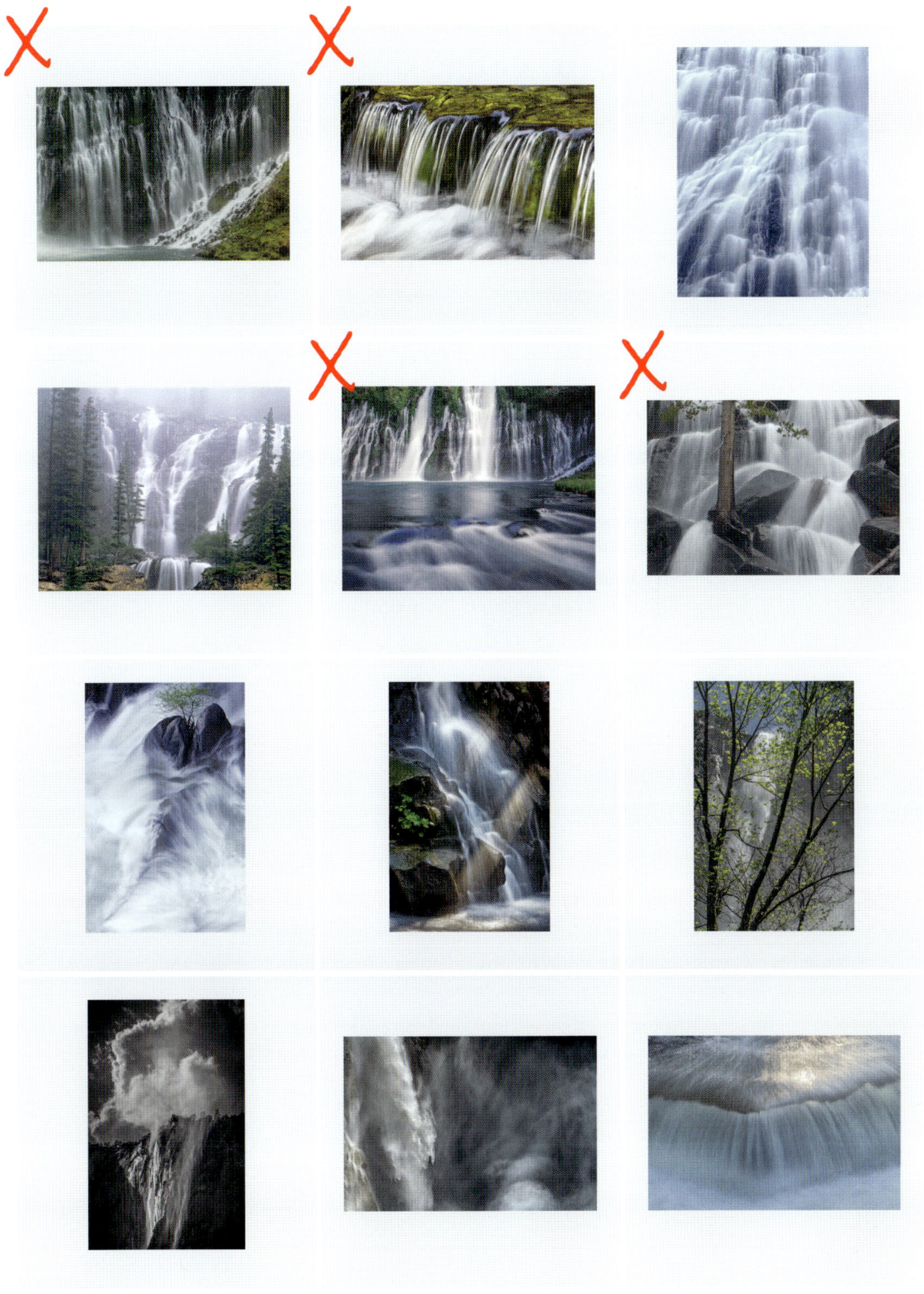

YOUR ASSIGNMENT: MAKE NEW PHOTOS FOR A THEME

For this assignment, we want to practice the ideas I've put forth by making all new images (not previously exposed images) with a clear theme in mind, then analyzing them using both technical and aesthetic criteria. You may use a theme from the previous assignments, but not images you've already chosen for them, for your Lesson Three Collection.

First, spend a little time looking at the images of others whose work you admire. Look through books, calendars, note cards, websites, etc., to find their images. Look around for new photographs of your favorite subjects, especially those related to the subject you've chosen for the assignment. Think about developing your visual literacy, and see what qualities are striking in photographs that excite you.

Decide on a subject for this assignment, and then make new images. While making use of your best photo technique, let your imagination go. Try all lenses and camera angles that come to mind. Crop in tight, move back, simplify, throw out of focus—have fun! But keep in mind that being creative does not mean being sloppy. Make use of all these ideas to zero in on what excites you about the subject.

Suggestions:

- Try to balance the time you spend making the images with the time you allow to process and curate them.

- As you edit your images, look carefully for a consistency of technical and creative qualities.

- I have often seen students compromising quality for content. If an image does not add content at a high-quality level, then you are working against the building process. You may not notice this quality-content imbalance initially, which happens to us all, but be vigilant!

Place up to ten images on your chosen theme into the Lesson Three Collection folder. These ten new images can be used to blend into your theme as you progress through these lessons.

YOSEMITE PORTFOLIO CASE STUDY

To illustrate how this assignment can be done, I am sharing my process through a one-day photo session in Yosemite Valley. To build upon the depth of my Yosemite archive, I recently spent some time making new work, just as I've asked you to do for this assignment. The first screenshot on the following page shows my narrowed-down selection of eighteen photographs. (See the introduction for more on this process.) I initially ranked images with stars, using a low number, to indicate that they passed my examination for technical and aesthetic quality.

I made 1,623 frames that day. The sunrise over the valley was spectacular, featuring extremely high-contrast light when aiming into the sun. I bracketed extensively to ensure that I captured the full range of details, especially in the deep shadows and bright highlights. All day long, there were clouds swirling around the granite cliffs. At mid-afternoon, the overcast weather softened the light and the wind died down, giving me a chance to photograph dogwood trees in full bloom. Even though the wind was relatively low, a slight breeze can ruin an exposure, so I made many frames to guarantee a few sharp ones.

As I compared and rated similar frames, the ones with the sharpest dogwood or the best array of clouds were ranked higher. I usually finalize the highest-ranked photographs in Photoshop, and when those are saved, they appear back in Lightroom and receive my highest five-star rating. Of the 1,623 images, 164 received three stars, 94 received four stars, and 32 five stars.

My final step for this selection process was to use color ranking, with "certain" images given the green light, and the "maybes" given the go-slow yellow mark. I found eighteen frames to give me a good range of subjects that I photographed that day. The first nine are sunrise, cloud-centric images made from iconic Inspiration Point. Since I have so many photos from there, I'm looking for a composition and lighting that is new and fresh for me. When you look at the second screenshot, you'll see I narrowed my selection down to four from that viewpoint (the other five are crossed out).

My final selection from this day is shown in the image grid on page 37. My choices were influenced by my long history in Yosemite and being aware of which frames might be redundant and not as good as previous photographs of that subject or location. My theme is the forthcoming Yosemite book, which will feature many new images—most likely these eight will be included.

When you decide on your theme or themes, you can focus your field sessions on the needs of that theme. Afterward, you can assess those new images and pull them into your Collection for that theme. As I've shown with my photos here, seeing the mixture of old and new for that theme, you can see what works and what doesn't, and what might be added in future field sessions.

In the second screenshot, you can see where I've edited images out with an X mark. The first group of nine images from Inspiration Point, Yosemite, was narrowed down to four. The ones eliminated

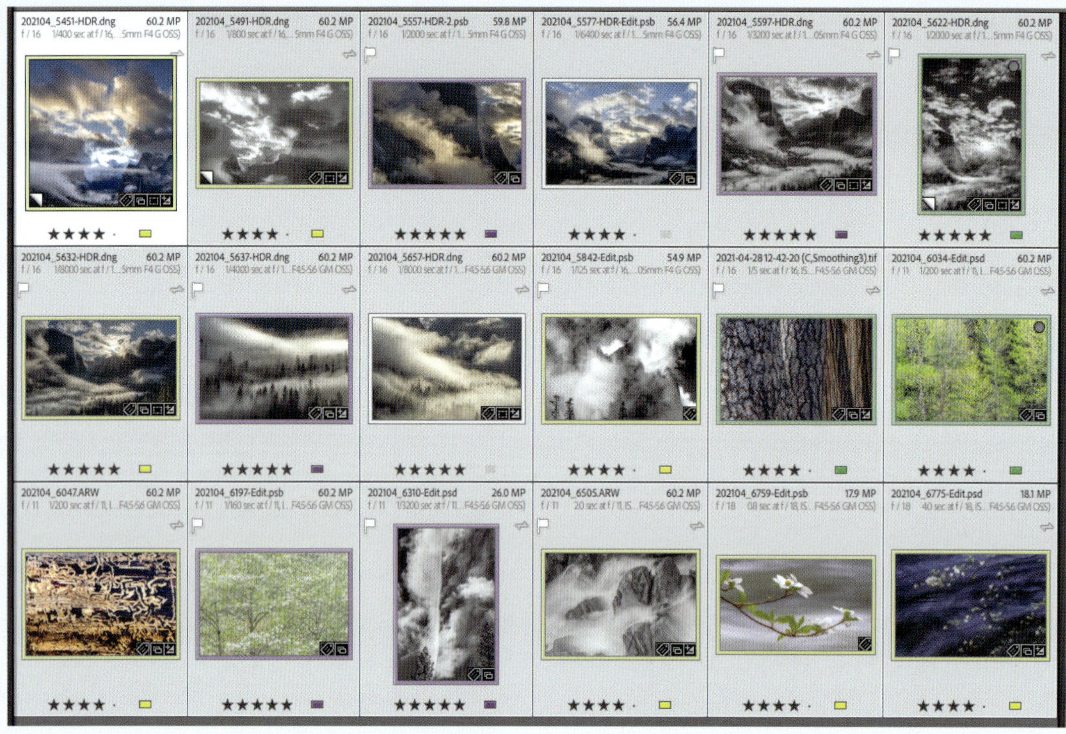

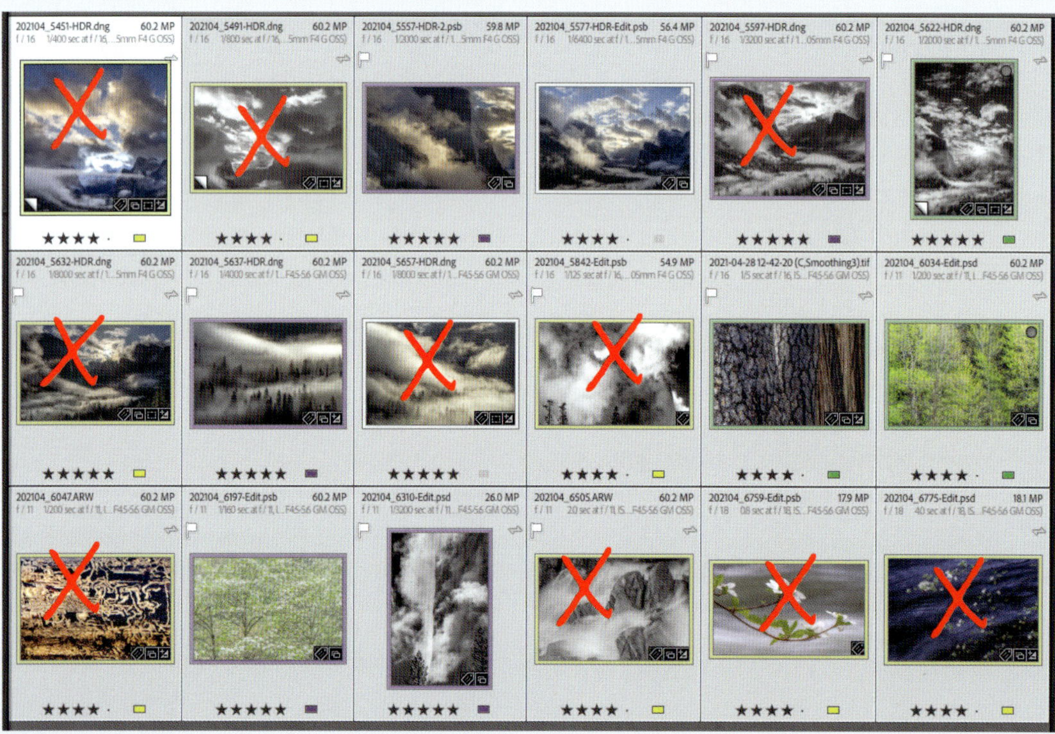

were X'd out based on several criteria: that I didn't want so many of the classic horizontal, wide-view images from the tunnel, my knowledge of other images of mine from the same location, and my subjective judgement that the ones I kept had even better light or more unique composition. Note my use of Green and Yellow ratings that help me keep track of the "likely" and "maybe" images.

Now you can see the results of how I narrowed my collection down from 1,623 images exposed on April 26, 2021, to eight finalists to be considered for the Yosemite book. Let this give you one approach to selecting your photographs for this assignment, and the upcoming ones.

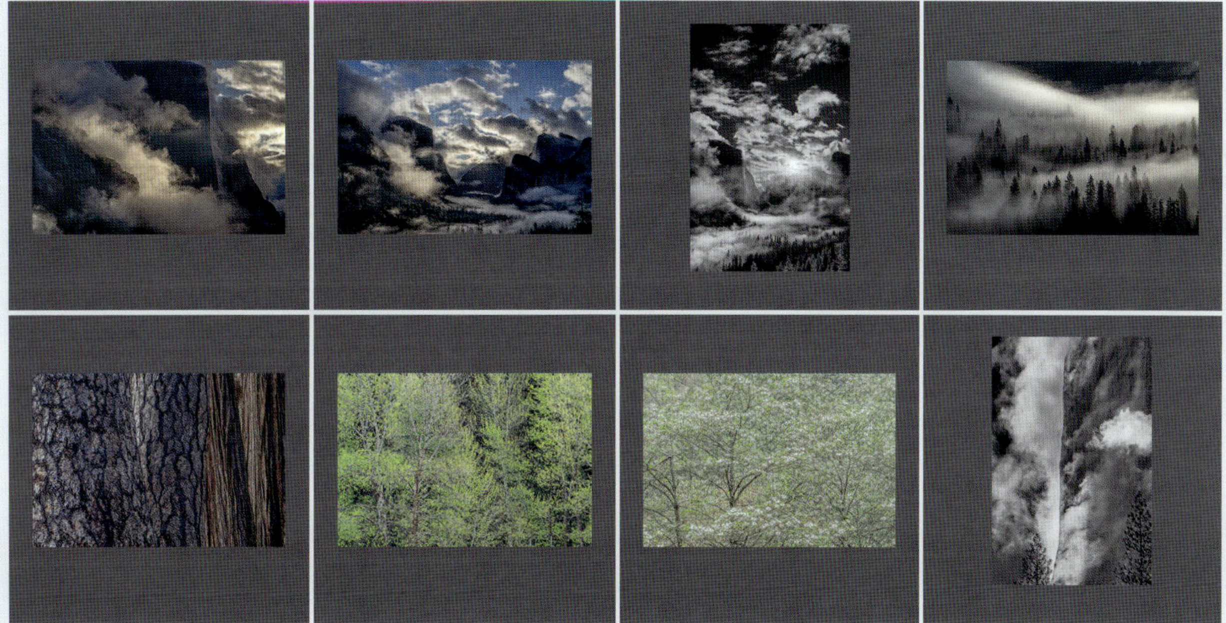

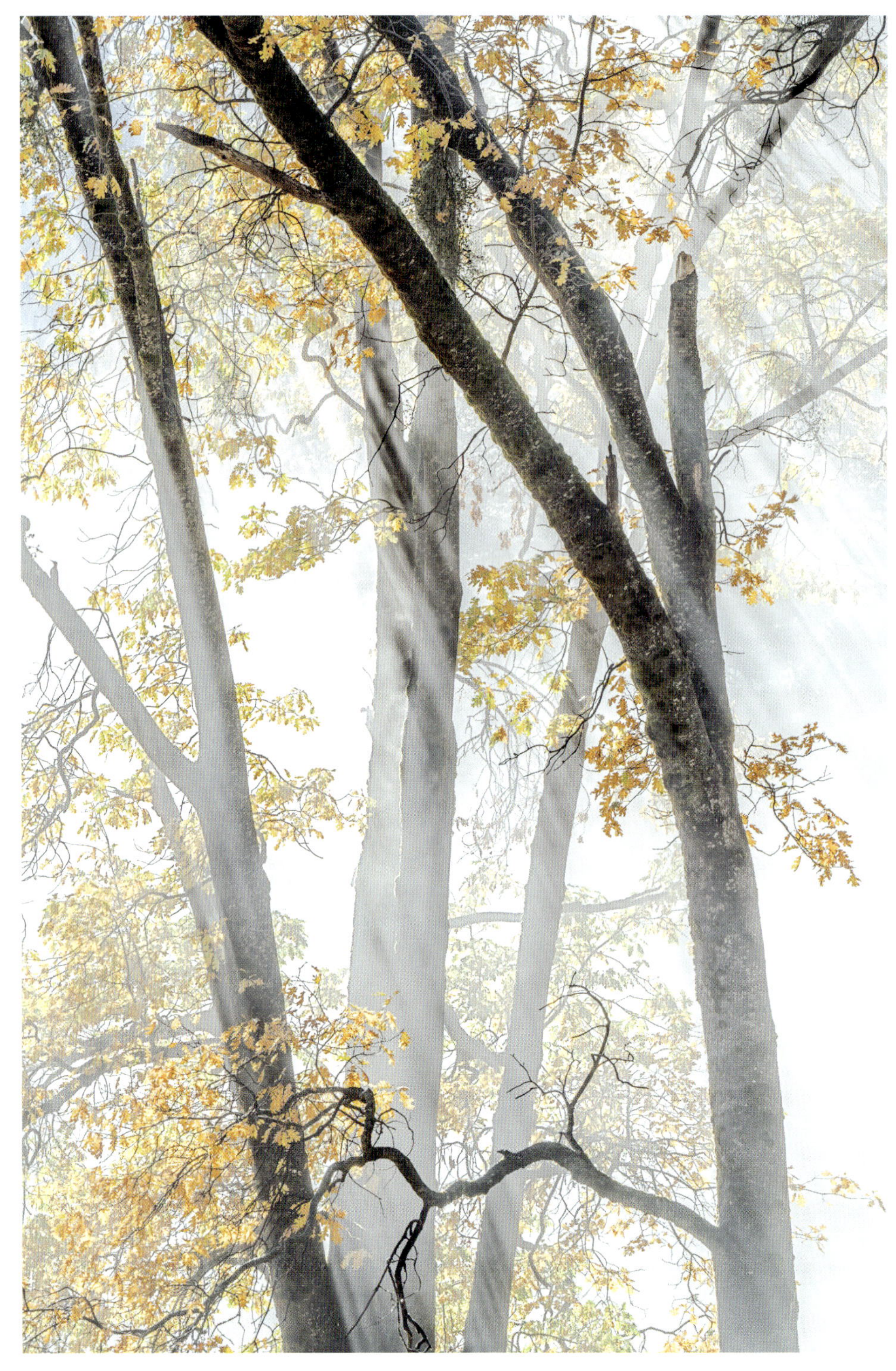

Oaks and Fog, Yosemite National Park, California, 2021

LESSON 4

BUILD UPON A THEME

OVERVIEW

The objective of Lesson Four is to build upon a portfolio concept with research into your archives and by assessing what new work might improve the whole. We also work on the idea of "context" editing for specific uses or types of clients.

ASSIGNMENT

Decide on a theme, then curate your collection(s) using both technical and aesthetic criteria. Begin the process of writing an artist's statement. (The assignment is described in more detail on page 45.)

In the first three lessons, I discussed in detail many ideas for and approaches to developing portfolios of your photographs. I've talked about the need for good editing to build a strong portfolio. Editing well is really the fastest way to improve your images. As you improve your photography, you can't really see the improvement if you can't organize and, in a way, document your progress. In the latter half of the book, we will be working on exercises to apply the ideas in the lessons. This is where practice becomes the main path to improvement. I used to tell my kids to remember this line from a Sesame Street song, "Practice, and tomorrow you'll be better than today!"

In this lesson, we begin the incremental process of building a theme. Deciding on a theme in this workshop, or in general, is often not a linear process. It is okay to shift themes as you progress, to a completely new idea or a refinement of where you started in Lesson Two, or by adding to the new work created in Lesson Three. As your skills develop, you will most likely become more efficient. You will discover that the process has its ups and downs, with changes of direction or speed of progress that are totally expected in this creative exercise. The art of blending images into a cohesive group takes much practice, so you will notice each of the following lessons involves additional refinement of your theme, ideally making the theme stronger each step of the way. NOTE: Making new work is always encouraged for each lesson.

EDITING BASICS REVIEW

First, let's review the main quality concerns to check when selecting portfolio photographs:

Check Exposure

Up to a point, the quality of an exposure is subjective, but if bright areas are overexposed or an important element is lost in an underexposed area, then the photograph belongs in the reject pile.

Check Sharpness

For digital images, inspect files at 100 percent. At 200 percent, no image will look sharp.

Check the Composition

Is the composition clean and the intended subject clearly defined? Are there distracting elements on the edges of the frame, or in front of or behind the subject?

Check the Content and Emotion

Does this photograph mean or say anything? About you? About the subject? Is it unique and creative?

ESTABLISH LEVELS OF QUALITY

When I edit my images, I always end up with different levels of quality at first. As much as I try to be a perfectionist, many of my photographs are just average. Most are technically fine. Most are sharp where they need to be sharp. Most of the time, the lighting is good. Ansel Adams once said, "Twelve significant photographs in any one year is a good crop."

Most of us would stop taking photographs if we came away with only twelve photographs a year to show for our efforts, ones that we wanted to show anyone. We all have tiers of quality in our work. If a portfolio is only a collection of the best images, usually grouped by subject or theme, where do all the other photographs go? We all have images that we wish to share, even if they are not perfect.

CONTEXT EDITING

What has worked for me is to apply what I call *context editing*. The ranking of my images depends on the context in which they will be used. For example, if I am curating my images for a calendar, which is often a retail product, my selection might include a broader range or quality of image standard. The grouping may include "top tier" photographs as well as more representational and typical compositions. All of these images will be of high technical quality and soundly composed, but some may be lacking a creative spark.

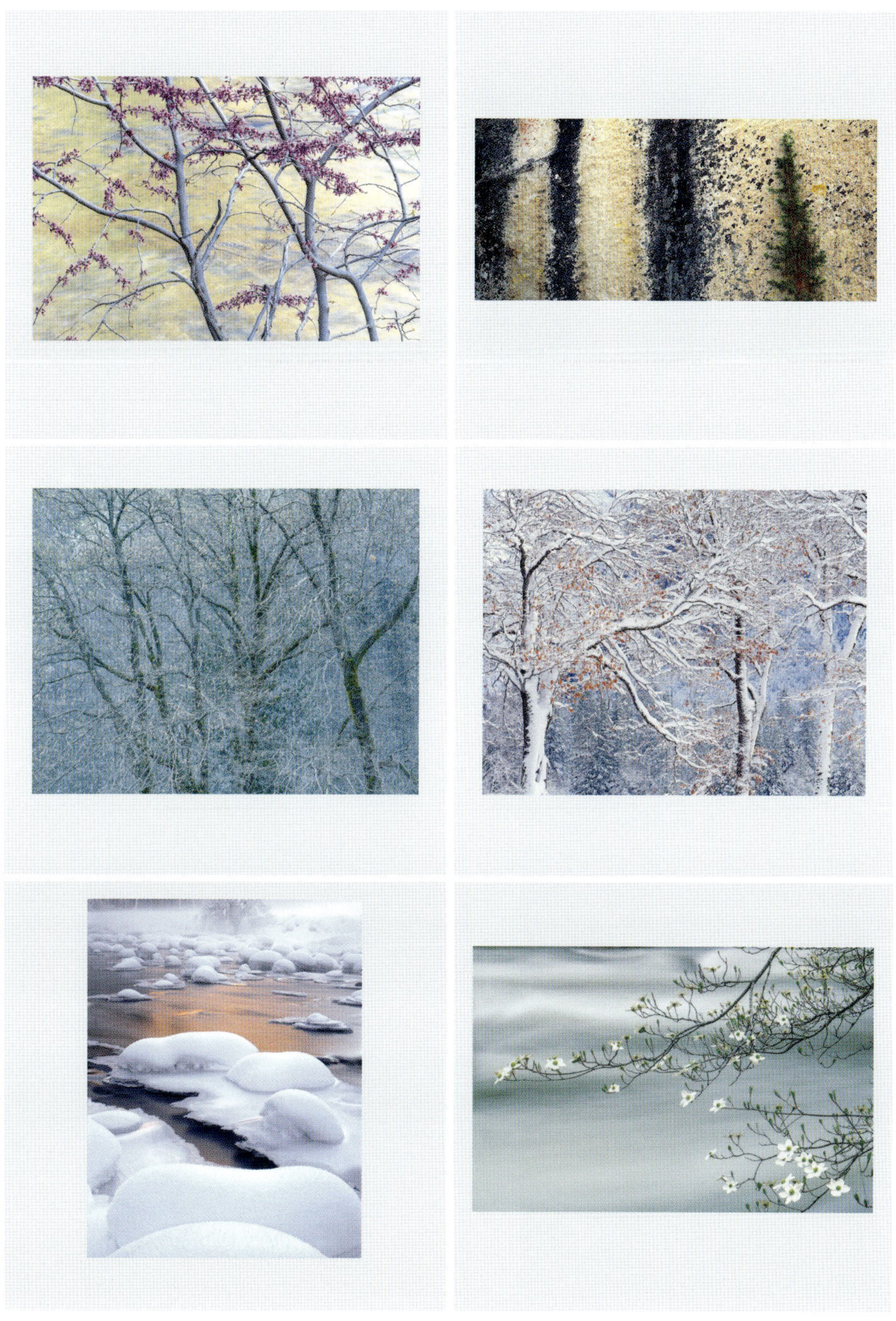

Here is a small selection of Yosemite images. The theme of this collection is "Intimate Yosemite." As a group, I feel that the images are on the same level in both quality and creativity. They are diverse in subject matter in a way that gives the viewer a personal, unique, and intimate view of Yosemite. This sample collection is a small illustration of a good balance of subjects, color, season, and quality.

My most creative images are often selected for more specialized and limited purposes. They are reserved for my fine art portfolio. They will appear in photography galleries selling my fine art prints, and in books and articles where I want my very best work represented.

Suppose that you are invited to show your wildlife photographs from Africa to a local conservation group. If the purpose of the presentation is educational, and the viewers are not photographers, you can show them your most artistic images plus some natural-history-based, descriptive pictures that will give them more information and a broader view of the locale. A similar thought process would be useful if you were to exhibit the same images at a natural history museum. If you are showing your portfolio to a fine art photography gallery, then only your finest, most creative images will do!

Let's say I am invited to participate in a national park exhibit at a fine art photography gallery, and I decide to include a photograph from Grand Teton National Park. Here are two images from which to choose.

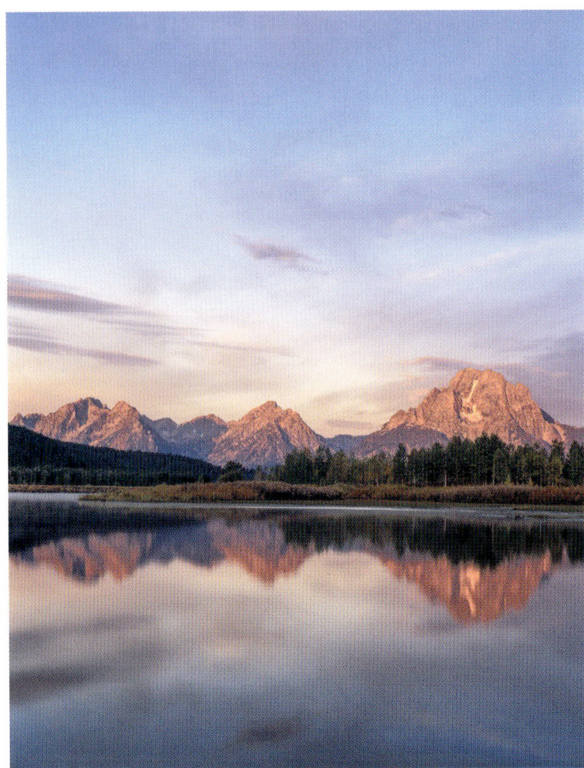

Reflections, Mount Moran, Grand Teton National Park, Wyoming

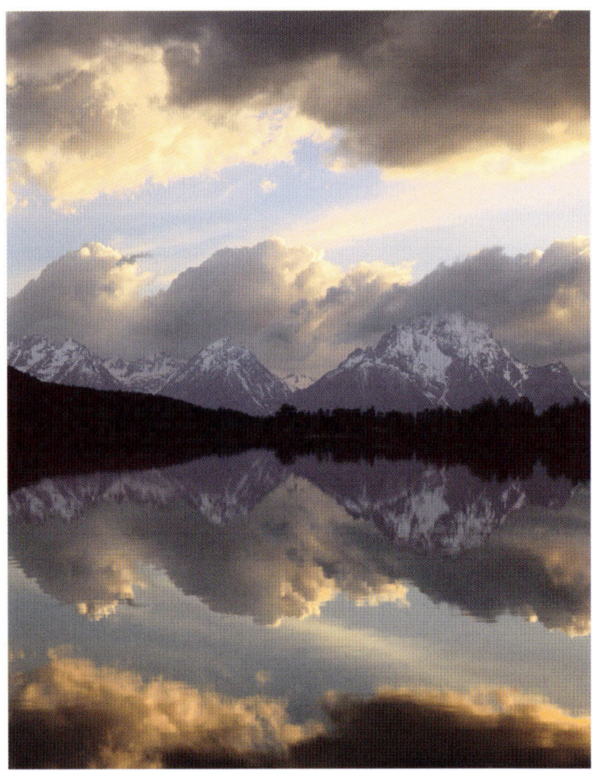

Cloud Reflections, Mount Moran, Grand Teton National Park, Wyoming

Given that the purpose of this theoretical exhibit is to feature my most interpretive national park images, one image is the obvious choice to me. My *Cloud Reflections, Mount Moran* photograph on the right is a much more evocative portrayal of this classic scene. It also exemplifies my personal style of photographing moody landscapes. While the *Reflections, Mount Moran* photograph is of good quality, it is more generic and less distinctive.

GROUPING BY QUALITY AND CONTEXT

Choose a context in which your portfolio could be presented. I often work with students who have an upcoming exhibit or a book idea they've had for years but never got started. Or the context could be updating a web gallery or delivering a proposal to a publisher. Collect your images, old and new, into a group that shows consistency of quality. Keep in mind that a variety of lighting types, location, scale, season, and subject matter will add depth to the portfolio.

If you feel that you need a new direction, choose a theme for which you have at least a few strong images, and then add new images to this new group.

Suggestion: Continue your research of photographs that fit into the theme you chose in Lesson Three to improve your visual literacy. Look in books and magazines, search the internet, or go to museums or galleries.

PHOTOGRAPHER'S STATEMENT

Once you've made your selection, I highly recommend that you write a brief essay, or photographer's statement, about the collection of images. This can be just a few sentences, or you can write more if you want to. Being concise is helpful—no more than one page of text is a good rule of thumb. Your words should define the goals for your selected theme or what inspires you about the theme.

This statement gives you the opportunity to address the potential viewer. Write as if you are introducing the portfolio to a new audience, as if they know nothing about you or your images. Imagine that you are writing an introduction to a book. This may prove useful if you choose to use a book as your final presentation form for Lesson Eight. If you were asked to exhibit your prints, an artist's statement or opening essay would likely be a requirement. The writing can take the form of a story about making the images in some creative way, a description of the mood or emotion that the work evokes in you, or even a poem. Whatever form it takes, try to relate your experiences to the viewer.

I realize that some folks don't feel comfortable or confident about such writing, but I feel that it is a good exercise for any portfolio's development, as it will help you define your interests and thought process. The writing process often stimulates ideas for theme titles and may help you think of photographs in your archive that you hadn't thought of previously.

MY PHOTOGRAPHER'S STATEMENT

The reason I photograph is to experience the beauty of Nature, of wild places. I explore the essential elements of rock and tree, of cloud and rushing water to discover the magic and mystery of the landscape. My search for beauty is a passionate and idealistic one. It is the spirit of the land I seek, be it in a small piece of urban wildness or in a vast wilderness. Rachel Carson, in her book *The Sense of Wonder*, writes, "Those who contemplate the beauty of the earth find reserves of strength that will endure as long as life lasts."

Photography is a quiet, intensely meditative activity for me. Minor White, the Zen-influenced photographer, stated, "Be still with yourself, until the object of your attention affirms your presence." When the light and the subject inspire me, I am compelled to compose an image. The images that I enjoy making the most are those that rely on emotional response and perception rather than the spectacle of the scene. I enjoy isolating the details of a scene, often to the point of abstraction. An intimate and enigmatic feeling can come through by creating photographs where the content or orientation is not obvious. I would rather make an image that asks a question than one that answers one, one that intrigues and arouses curiosity in the viewer.

What little wilderness is left on earth will be lost if we don't develop a new and enlightened environmental stewardship where Nature and Man are not considered separately. Barry Lopez writes, "Wild landscapes are necessary to our being. We require them as we require air and water. But we need, at the same time, to create a landscape in which wilderness makes deep and eminent sense as part of the whole, a landscape in which wilderness is not an orphan."

Perhaps one way the world will change is for people to go through a profound aesthetic experience that makes us aware that we are personally accountable for our actions and how we affect the environment. I can only hope that my photographs can provide such an inspirational experience and convey an enduring sense of wonder, a deep appreciation of the magic, beauty, and mystery of the natural world.

▶ As an example of my editing process, this selection shows a core group of photographs for my Antarctic Dreams portfolio. As I progressed through the thousands of images I made on that trip, I built out from the core to add new work that met my quality level established by this group of images. My curation resulted in an eBook and Blurb hardcover book (see Lesson Seven).

YOUR ASSIGNMENT: BUILD UPON A THEME

For this assignment, the goal is to practice the ideas I've put forth here with a clear theme in mind, then curate your collection(s) using both technical and aesthetic criteria. Decide on a subject for this assignment, and either make new images or add photographs from your archives (ideally, you'll do both!). Again, you may decide to refine one of the themes you have been working with in previous lessons, or you may pick an entirely new subject. The most efficient route is to select the theme you've already been working on. Be willing to make mistakes. Dig into your existing library to seek out those images that fit the theme and also maintain a high quality. Make use of all these ideas to zero in on what excites you about the subject.

I recommend that you begin the process of writing an artist's statement. Make notes regarding goals, jot down adjectives that express what you want your photographs to say. As concepts coalesce, notes or first sentences will develop into the full artist's statement. This will come up again in the Lesson Seven assignment.

Select up to thirty images (both existing and new) on your chosen theme to place in your Lesson Four Collection folder. Please select a title for your theme.

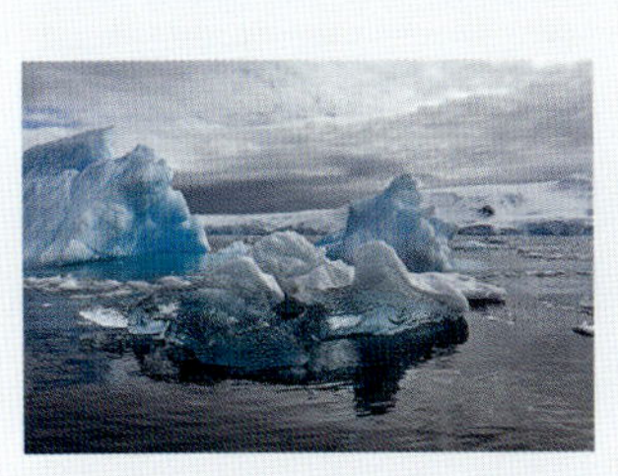
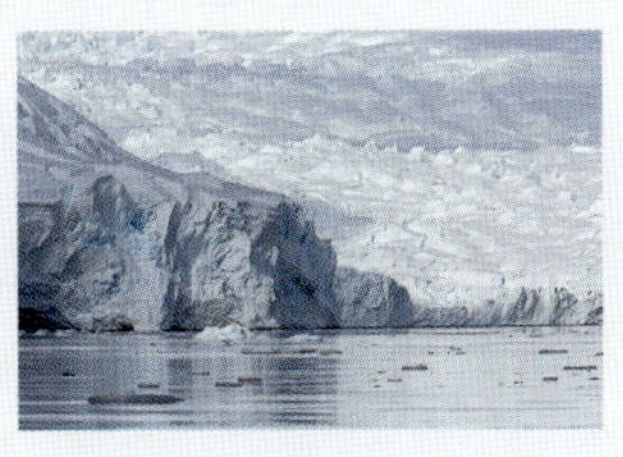
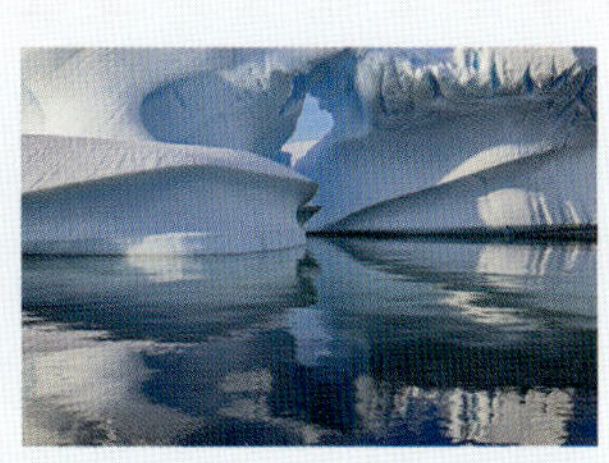
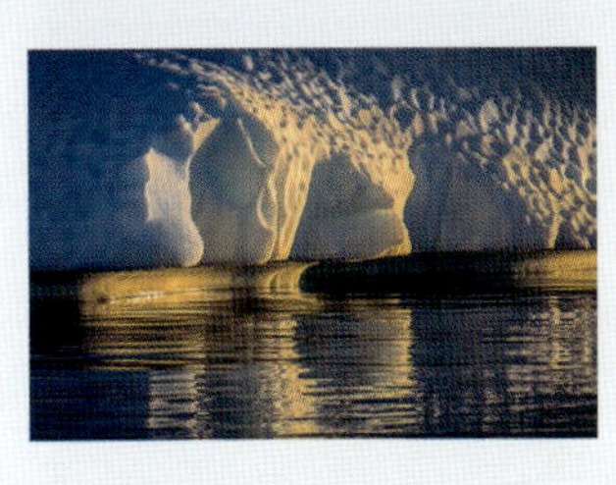
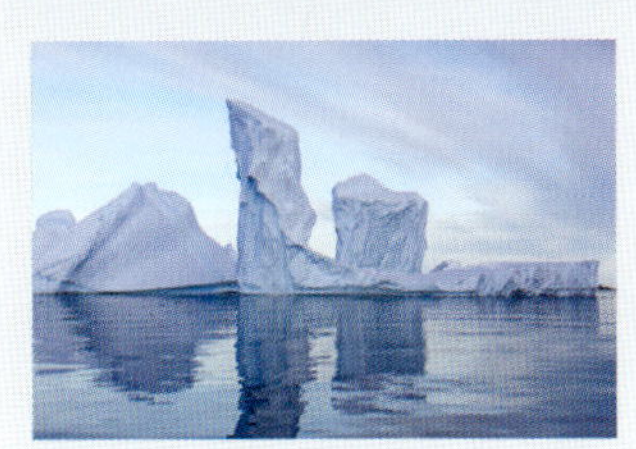
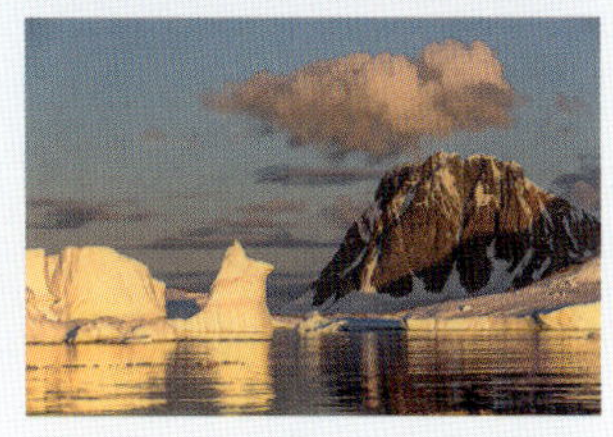

YOSEMITE PORTFOLIO CASE STUDY

In this sample of Yosemite photographs, I have selected images taken in high-country areas of the park. While a large number of photos in the book I am creating will have been taken in the Yosemite Valley area, I want the high country to be strongly represented. To demonstrate how I might complete this assignment (though here I'll pick only ten images), I am showing my first initial choices, which I use to get myself started without too much deliberation. In the screenshots, you can see which images I've X'd out, and I'll briefly give you the reason for each:

- #1: I want to include only images within the park's boundary. This first image was taken outside the park.

- #2: This image was removed because it was made outside the park, and it does not fit the overall "intimate landscape" style I want for most of the book.

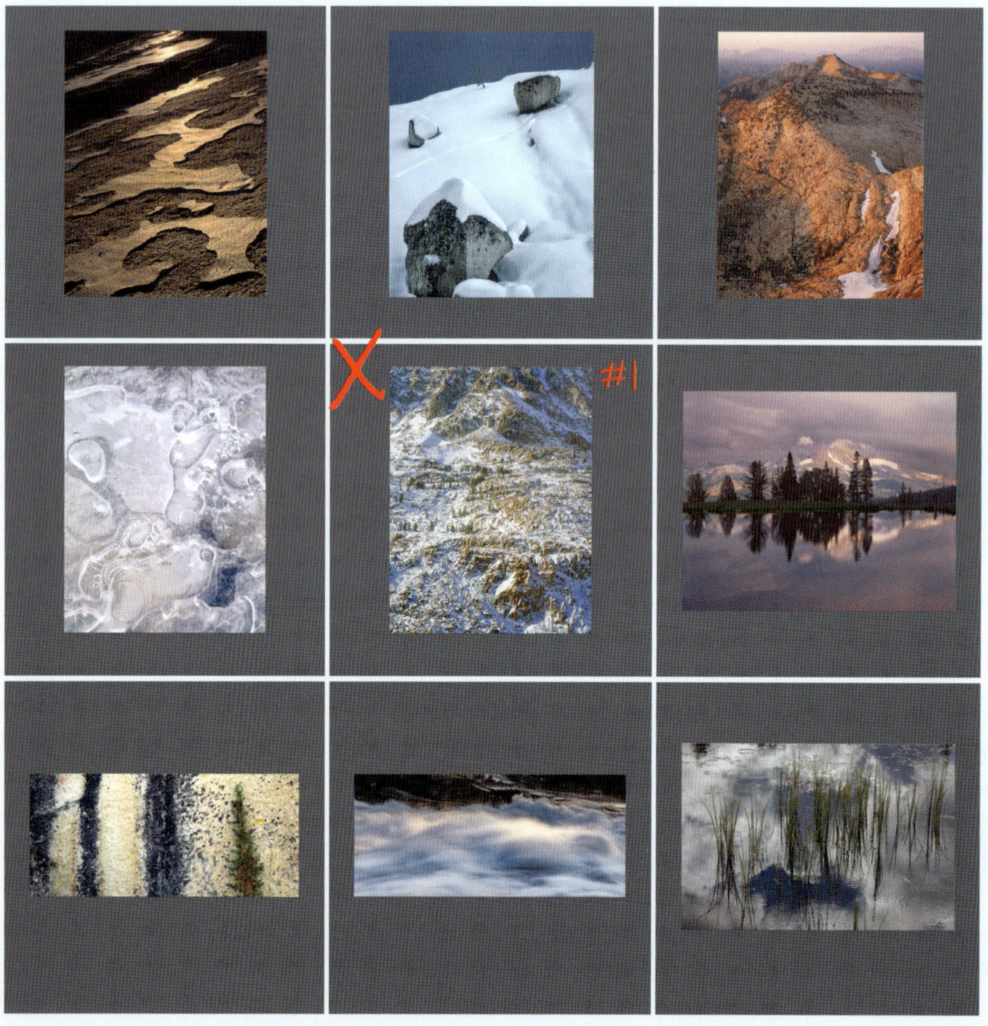

- #3: I really like this image, but this location is often photographed, so it's not especially unique.

- #4, #5, and #6: These are classic Yosemite subjects that have been published often, and I prefer to focus my book on images of subjects that are less known, quieter, and more subtle.

- #7 and #8: The final three photos represent the lush, green foliage of summer, so I grouped them together for comparison's sake. After looking at the group more closely, I selected the first one and removed the following two photographs.

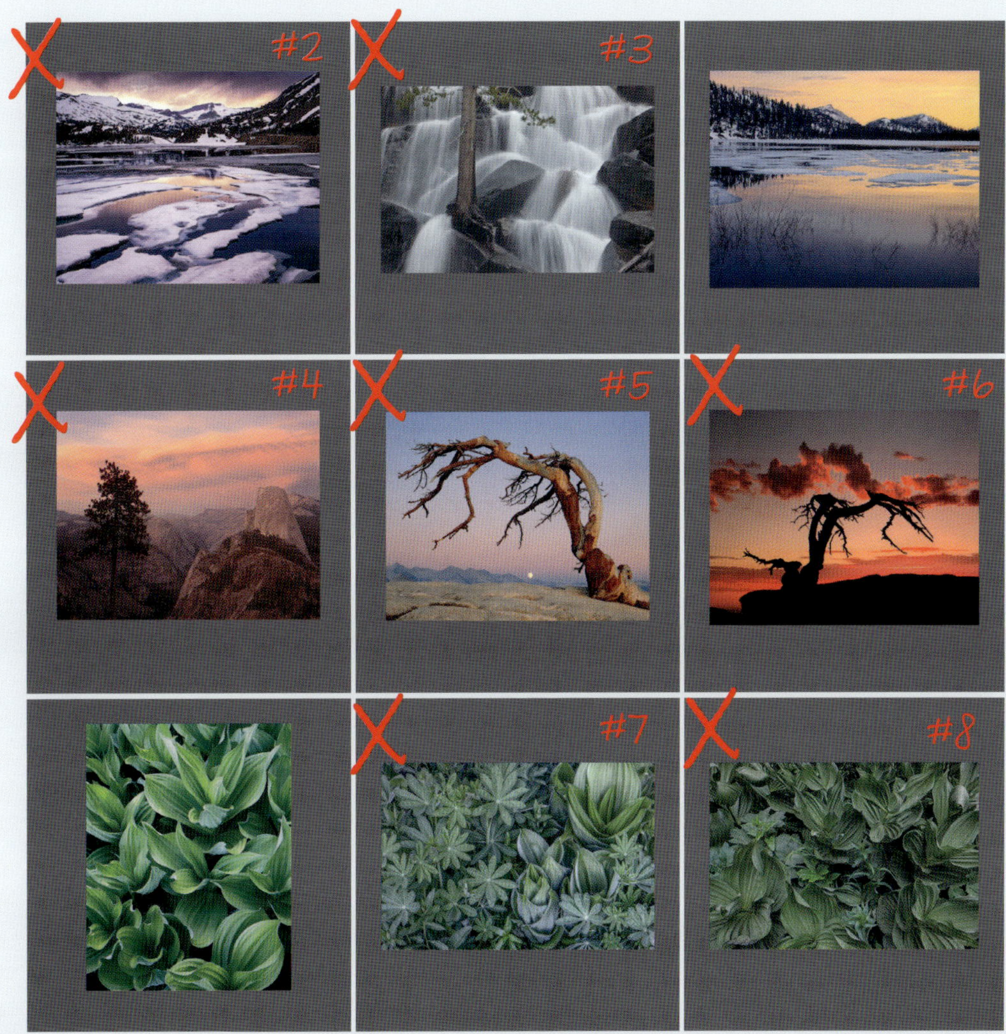

These are the final ten photographs that I feel reach my quality standards and fit well into the concept for the book.

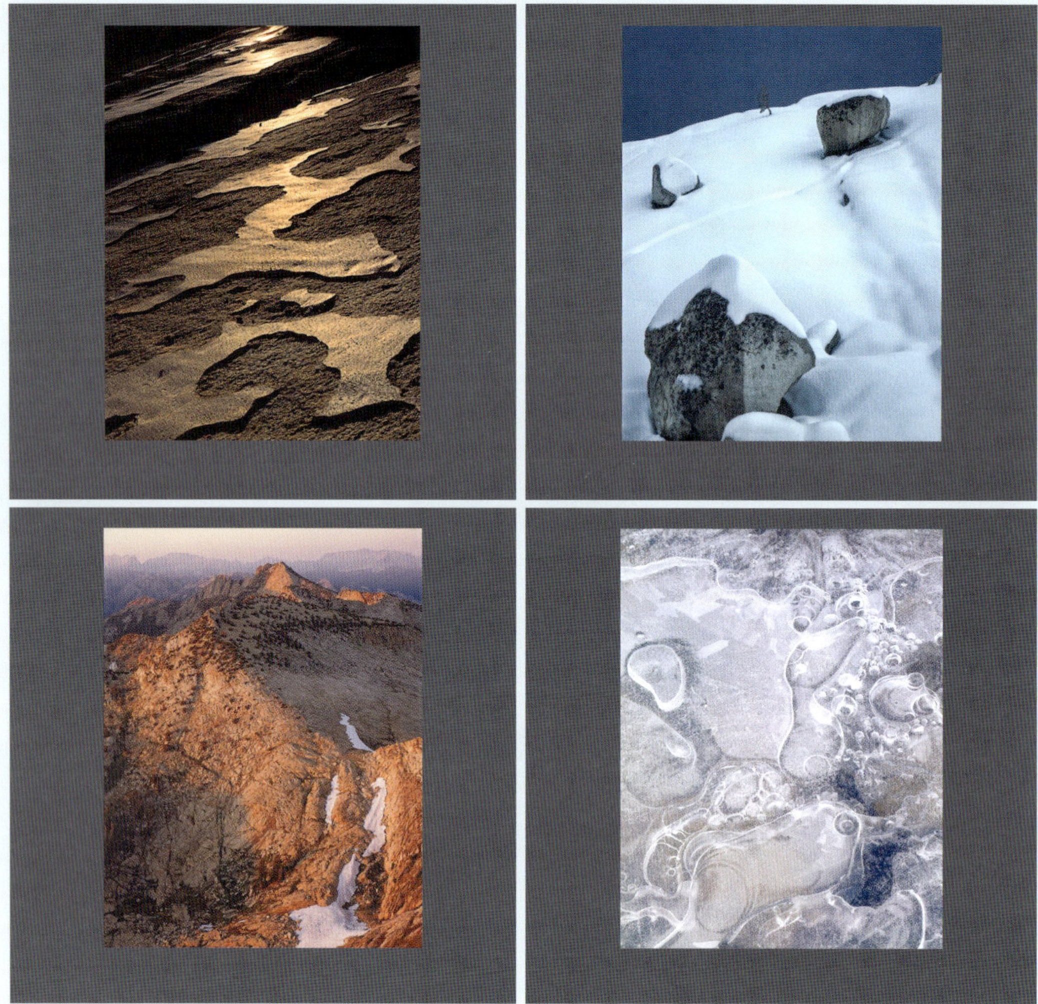

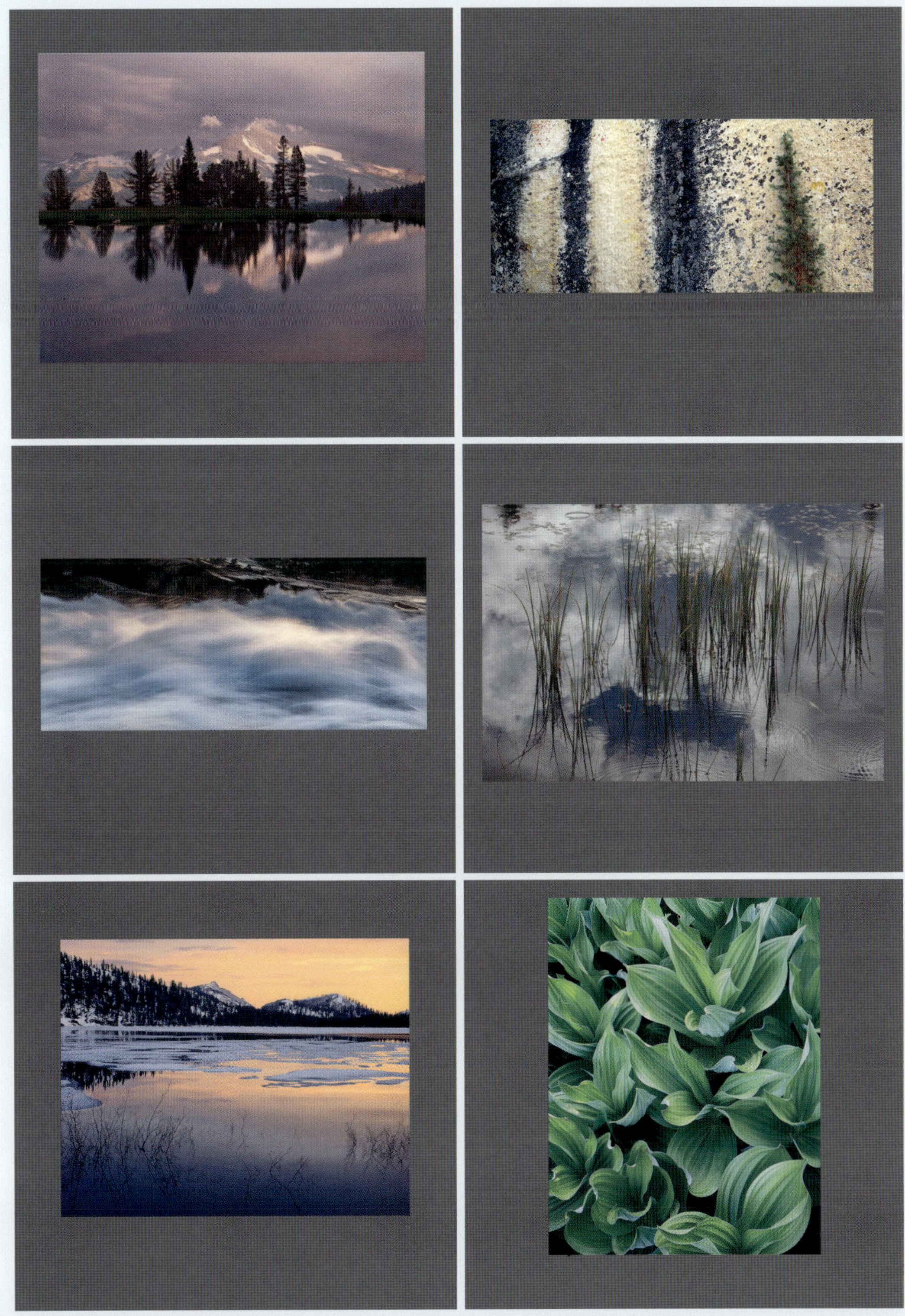

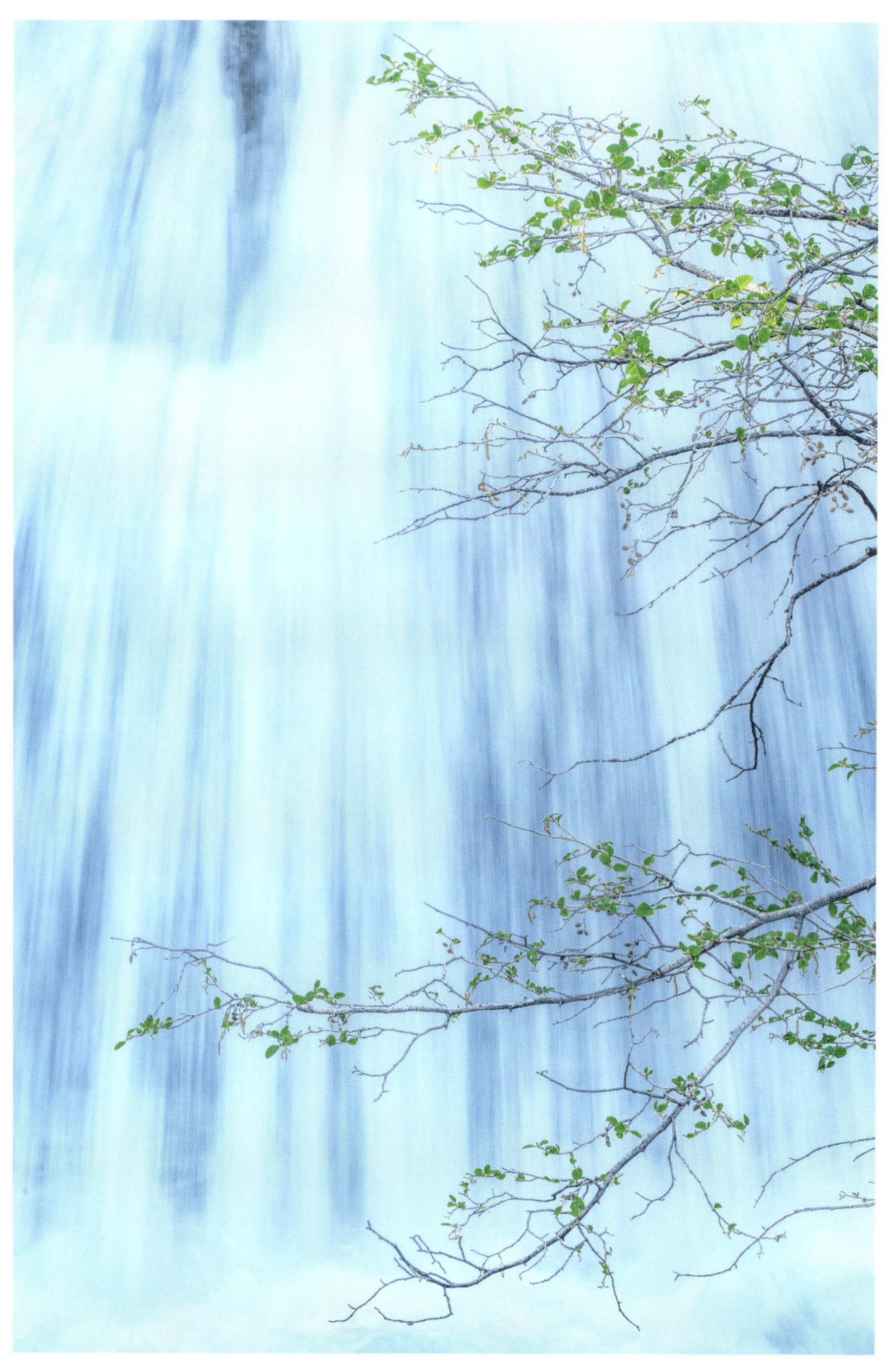

Alder and Waterfall, Yosemite National Park, California, 2021

ADD DEPTH TO YOUR PORTFOLIO

OVERVIEW

The objective of Lesson Five is to focus on creating depth in your portfolio by adding more photos, whether these are newly taken images or photos pulled from your archives.

ASSIGNMENT

Choose one of your established themes and photograph specifically with that theme in mind. Select ten to twenty images, including at least two new images, that blend harmoniously with the existing images in your portfolio. (The assignment is described in more detail on page 60.)

As you are editing new images, you should start to see more clearly what we have worked on previously. At this point, you should have:

- Explored what themes you have in your files;

- Learned to organize images based on a theme;

- Established a standard of quality (which you now have to live up to!);

- Researched other photography with the same themes that interest you, and improved your visual literacy;

- Examined the possible contexts in which you might use your images.

You are now gaining experience photographing and curating your images based on a theme (for which you have existing images) in mind. Remember the feedback loop we discussed in Lesson Three:

- Benchmark (standard of quality based on existing work)

- New work

- Assessment

- Add successes to portfolio

- Reject lesser images

- Learn from successes and rejects

- More new work

PRACTICE

Nothing can improve your photography more than practice and hard work, including editing and organizing your images. Practice is the process of becoming ready to make a great image or pulling together an exciting theme that adds depth and meaning to the individual photographs within a collection. Those past experiments and failures—the mental calculations for exposure, setting up your tripod quickly before the light changes, knowing how to refine a composition from many years behind the camera and in front of the computer—all have a cumulative value.

There are no shortcuts for the experience that allows you to be instinctive. After many years of work, decision-making can become intuitive, and your own vision has a chance to surface. Intuition, not technology or gadgetry, is the key to vision.

Nothing can improve your photography more than practice and hard work.

Even when this building process repeats, the group of images you are analyzing changes in what can seem to be imperceptible steps, but as you progress through these lessons, when you get to the end, I predict you will see very perceptible improvement. Once you are comfortable with the process, there is no reason the growth process can't be continued over months and even years.

REMEMBER: Editing is a skill—much ignored in instructional books—just as exposure control, or composition, or depth-of-field management are skills.

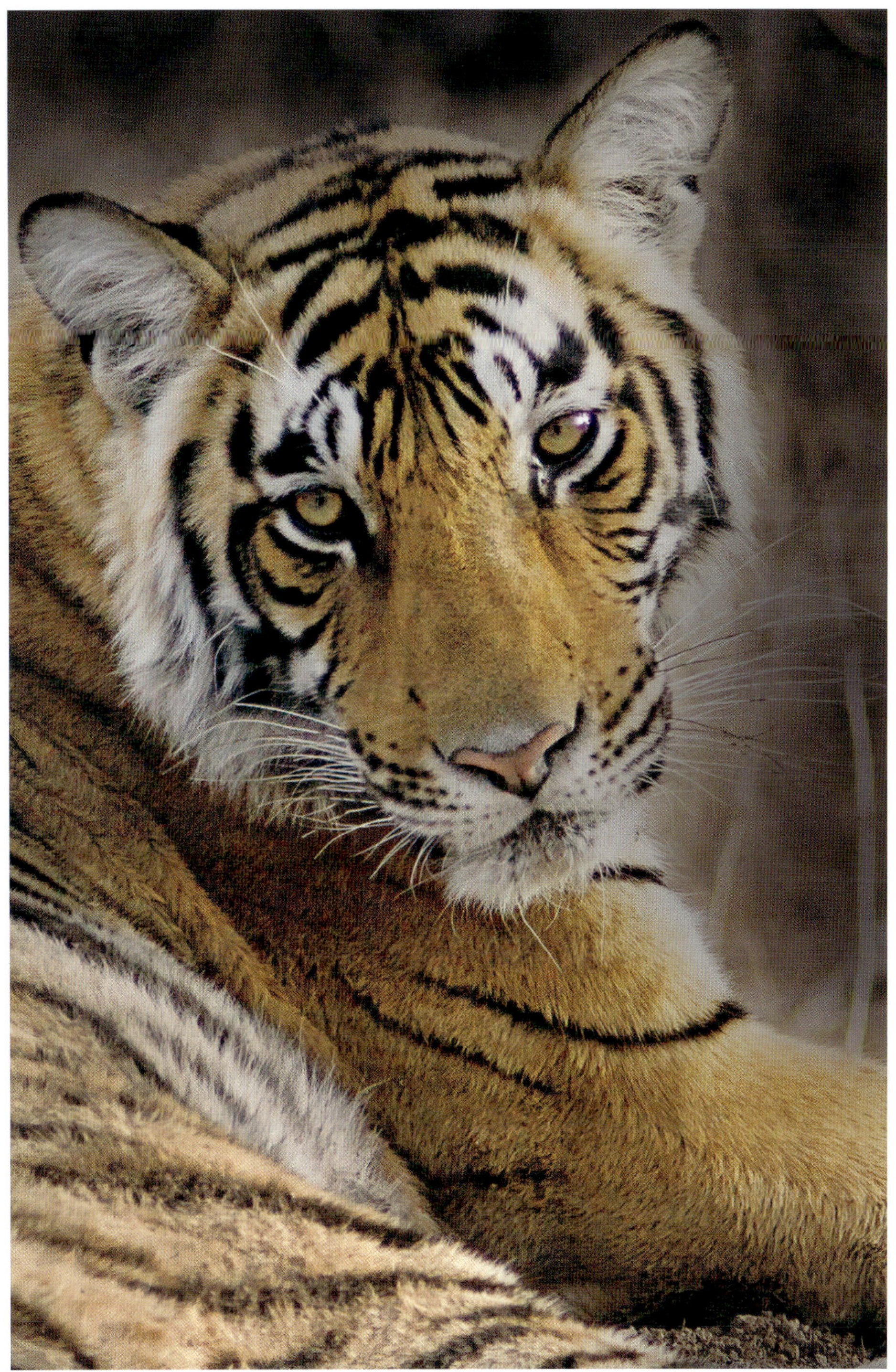

Tiger, Ranthambore National Park, Rajasthan, India, 2004

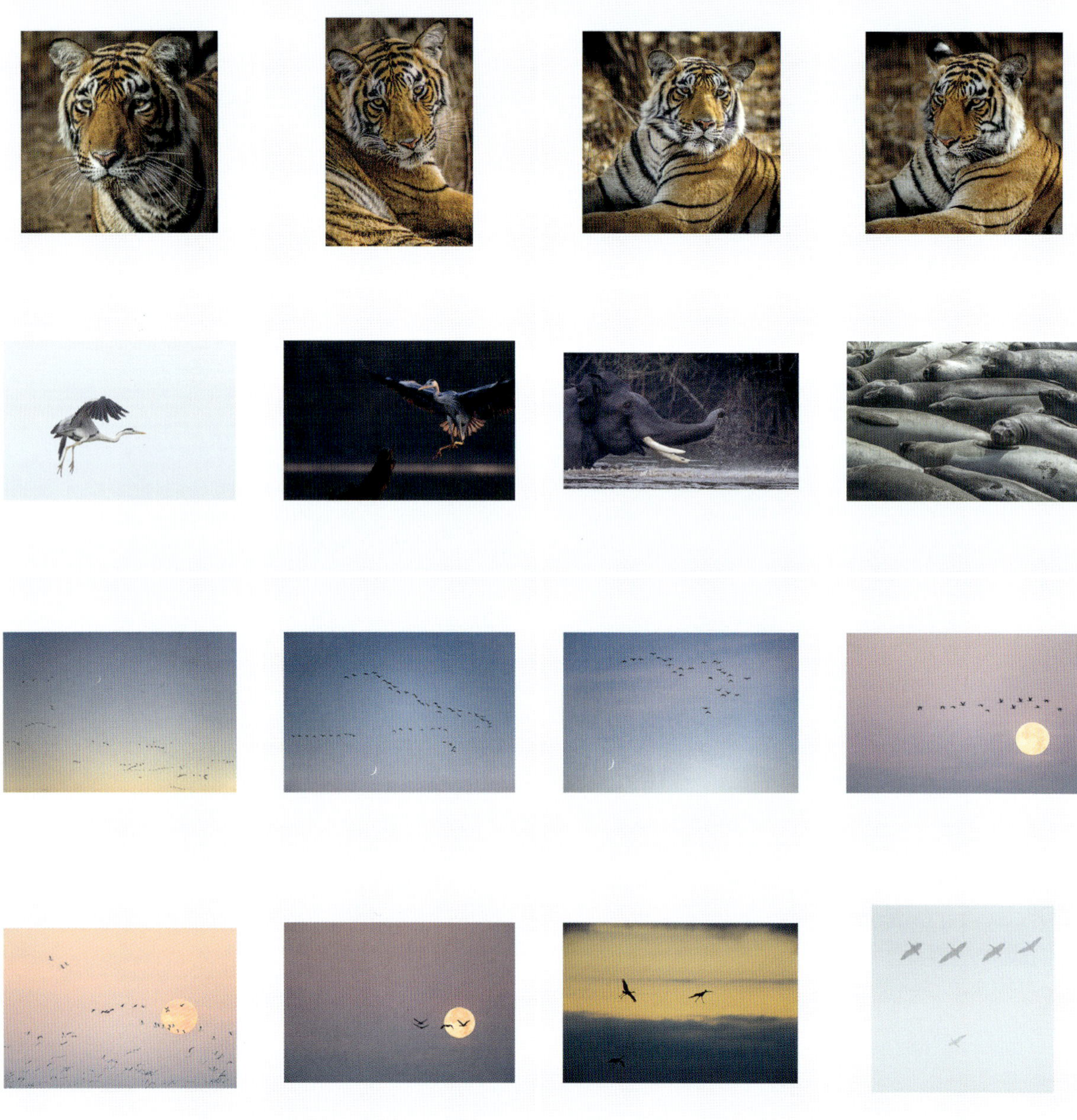

As an example of my curation process, I am going to create a small wildlife portfolio for my website. I don't often share these images, but I pride myself in having a diverse body of photographs beyond my usual landscape images. My context here is to create a tight selection for my webpage. My initial selection, shown here, is intentionally broad and includes work from India, Antarctica, and California.

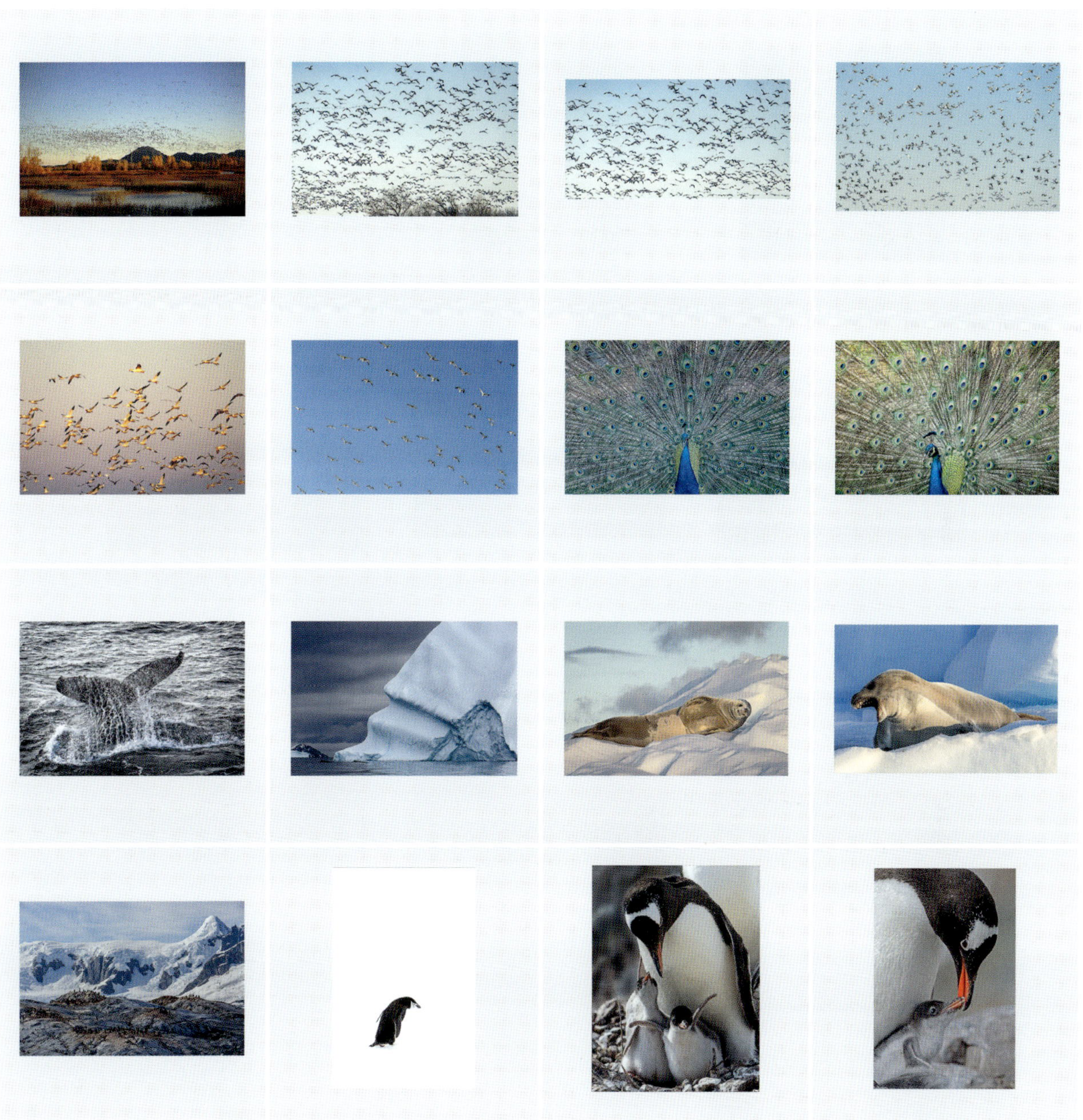

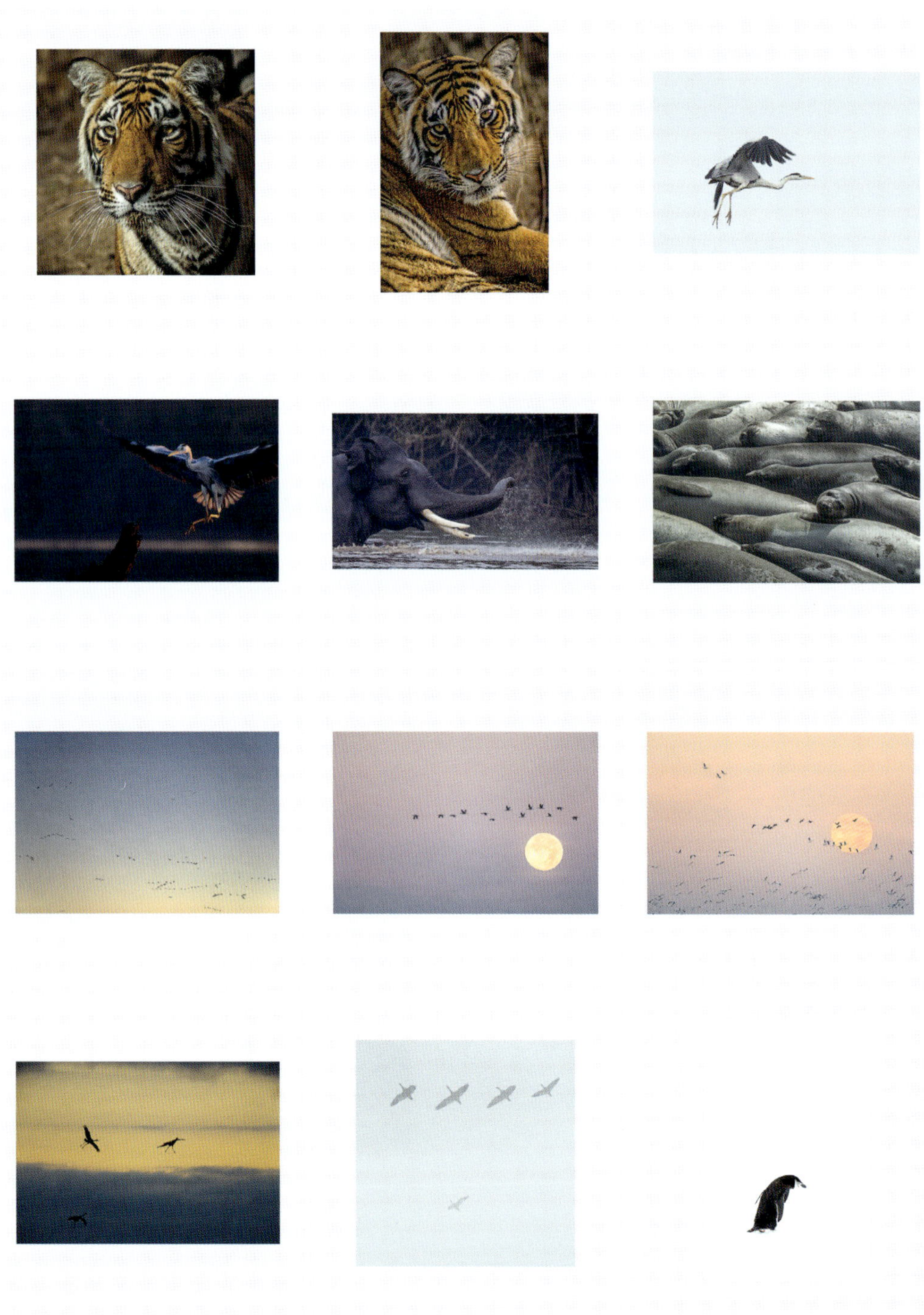

I've moved images around in the collection by type or subject. I put the tiger photos, the Antarctica ones, and the "birds in flight" together to help me visualize the strengths and weakness of the group.

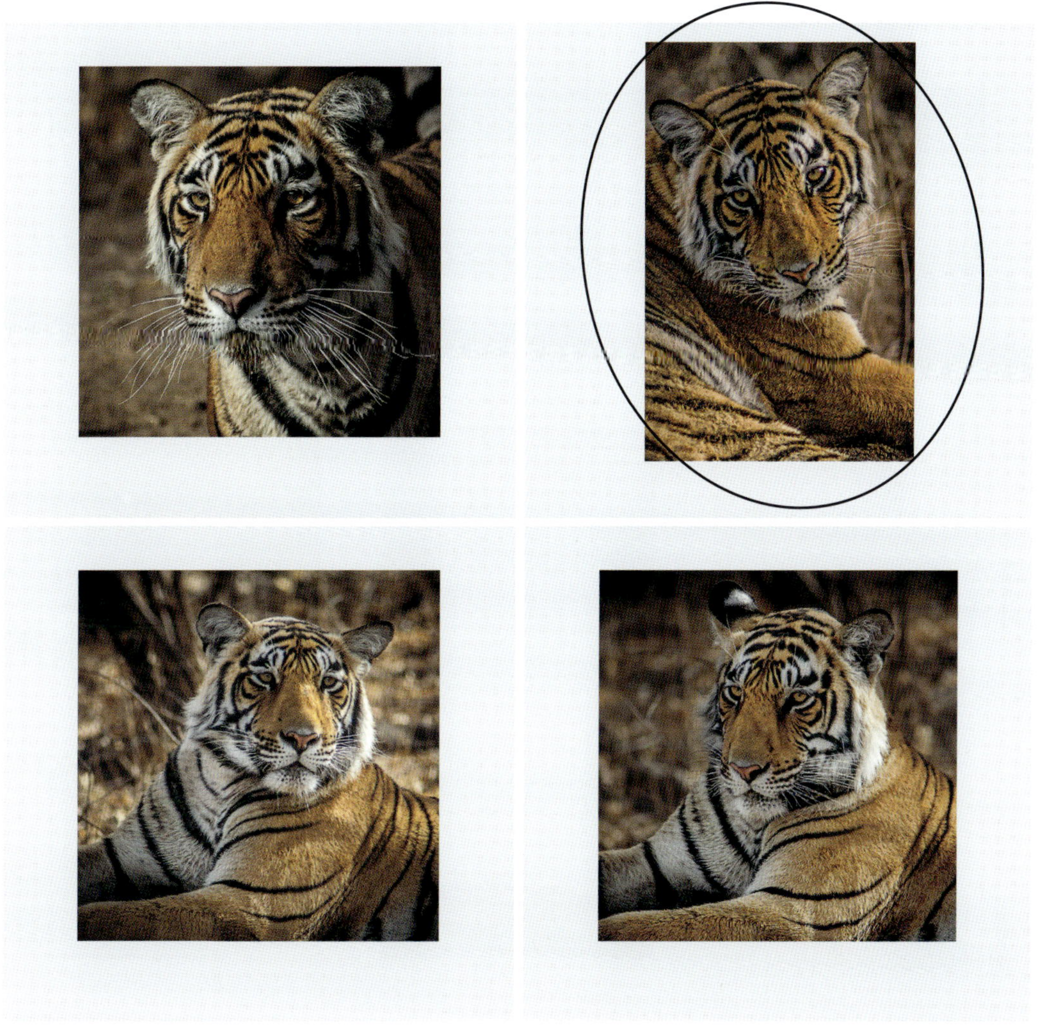

Now, using the Survey mode in Lightroom, I've grouped the tiger images together, and once I do, I notice that one photo stands out for me. The circled image is very similar to the others, but it includes eye contact, which makes all the difference to me. For the web portfolio, I don't want to show too many frames of the same subject. However, for other contexts, I could show more; for example, if I were submitting images to an editor, I may want to give them more choices for their usage.

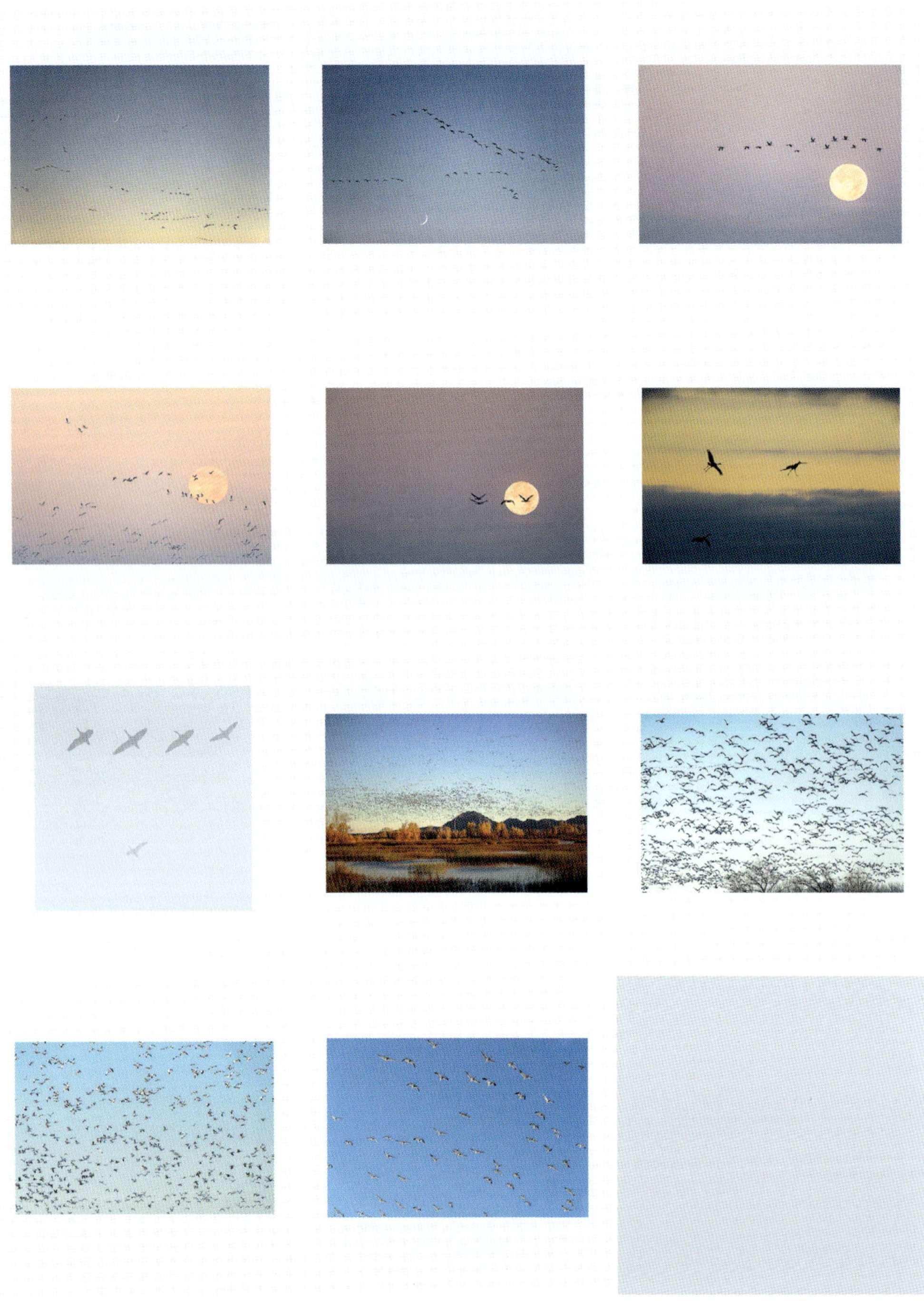

Here is a subset of bird photos I've made over the years in the nearby migration flyway of California's Central Valley. Looking at the group of five images featuring the moon and birds in flight, I notice the different colors of the sky and density of the birds. I need to pick two or three of them, as I feel five "moon and birds" is too many, especially when they are similar.

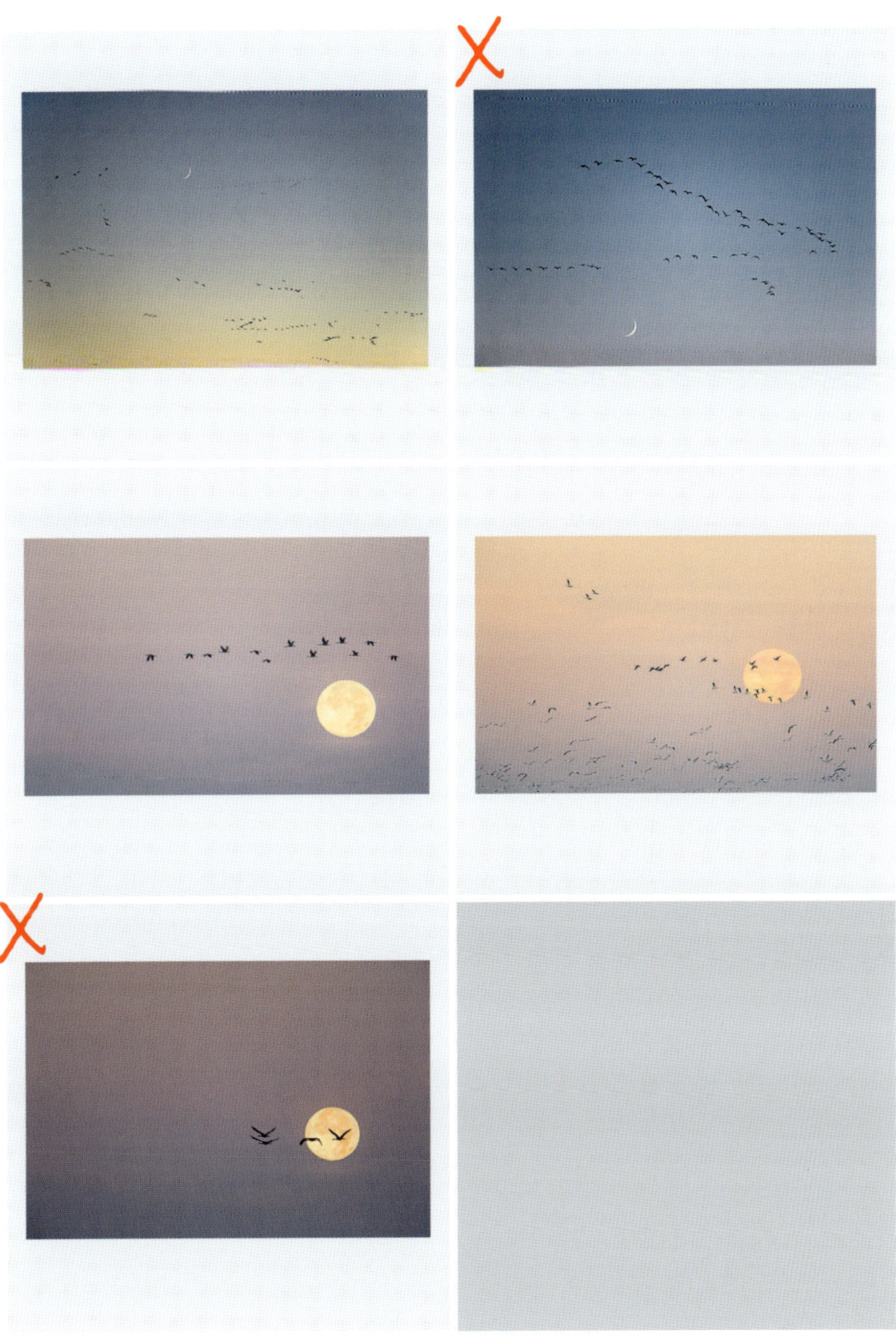

The top right frame shows the same moon phase as the top left frame, which has more exciting light with the gradation of color in the sky. The bottom image is an experiment in blending two frames taken a few seconds apart, which added a bird to the composition. I very rarely composite images together and don't wish to mix single-exposure frames with composited photographs, so I decided not to include this one.

YOUR ASSIGNMENT: BUILD DEPTH

Choose one of your established themes and photograph specifically with that theme in mind. Add at least two new images to the grouping that blend harmoniously and work well with your existing portfolio. Think about where to go photograph and what elements will add depth to your group, but don't have too tight a script. Better photographs come to those who wait, those who accept what opportunities come along. Place ten to twenty images (including both new and existing photos) on your chosen theme into the Lesson Five Collection folder.

Suggestions:

- Consider the "story line" of your theme. In other words, what are you trying to say about your theme? Think about what subjects will illustrate your story. Assess what you have already in your Collection that have met your quality standards, then make note of what other subjects might add depth. If your theme is based on landscape photography, consider if you have enough images of various seasons, or variety of scale, or if you have covered enough of the key elements of that landscape.

- Don't force new images into a portfolio. It is better to add one or two than dilute the group with many weaker images. Adding none is OK too in real life, but not so practical or educational for this exercise.

- Give yourself time to consider your choices, if possible. Although we can look at groups of images on our computers, like with the Survey mode, many pros like to make actual prints to view and assess, and lay out the prints for sequencing or grouping. Ansel Adams always talked about making prints and then placing them out where he would see them often. Come back to them often over a few days. If some still hold your interest, then group the new one(s) with the "selects," be it work prints tacked on your wall or thumbnails on your computer screen.

- Recognize that, if you've given yourself a schedule for this course, creating new photographs that qualify for your portfolio is difficult. Creative inspiration ebbs and flows, as I am sure you have experienced. Do your best in the time allowed. This is practice!

YOSEMITE PORTFOLIO CASE STUDY

I have an excellent new group of images I made during the spring of 2021, and to expand my spring selection for my Yosemite book, I first want to see a selection of my favorite Yosemite spring images from past years.

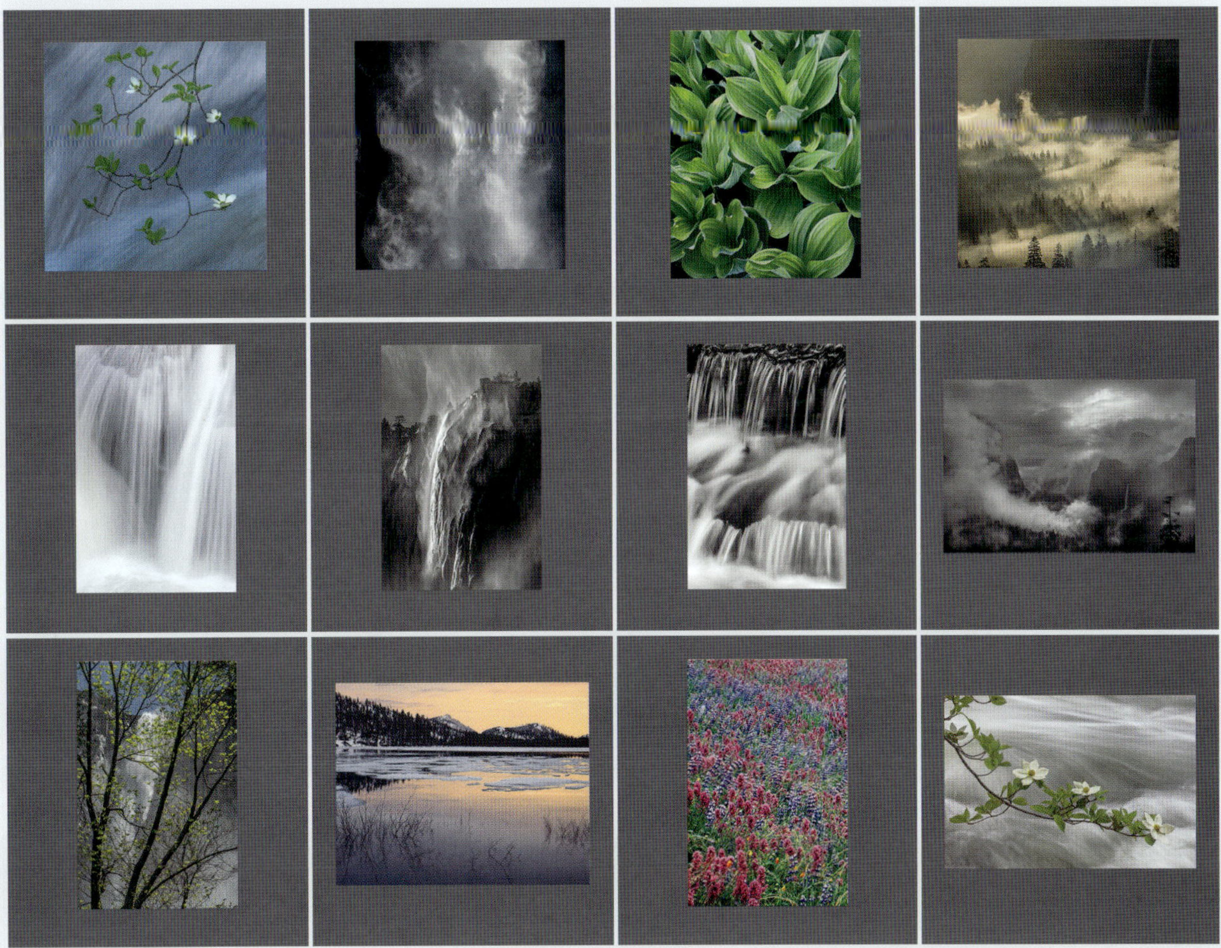

Here is a selection of Yosemite spring images I've created over many years that are under serious consideration for my book. Seeing this group is a starting point, a visual foundation to build upon with new work.

Next, I will pick my best photos from spring 2021 (below).

Then I will put them all together, old and new, in my collection (opposite page), and review them in Survey mode.

While I have mixed landscapes and isolated details with different perspectives, the quality remains consistent. There can always be debate as to favorites within any selection. Your choice may not be my choice, and ultimately the decisions must come from the artist. I learned a long time ago to tighten my edits for collections I submit to publishers to get their attention more successfully.

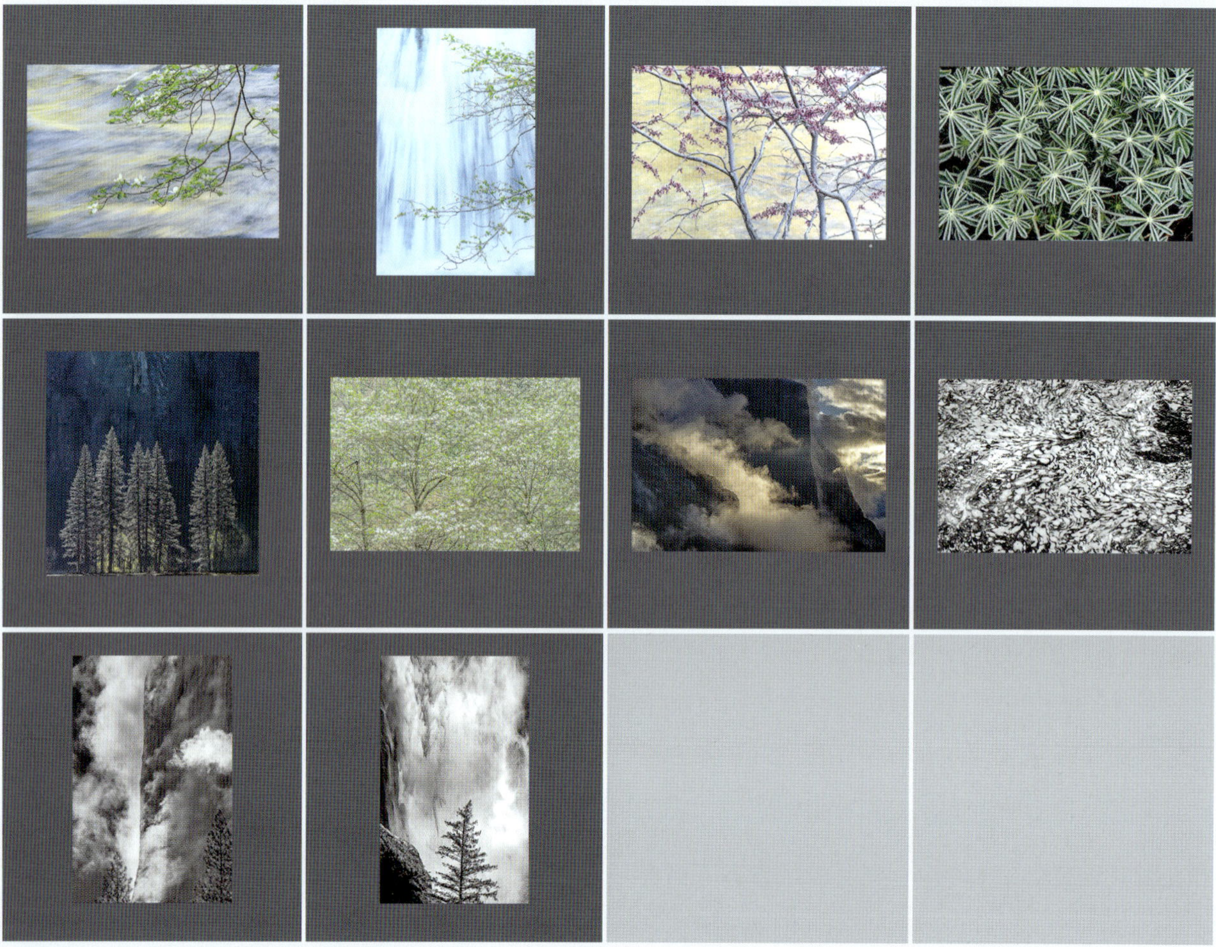

My top picks from Spring 2021.

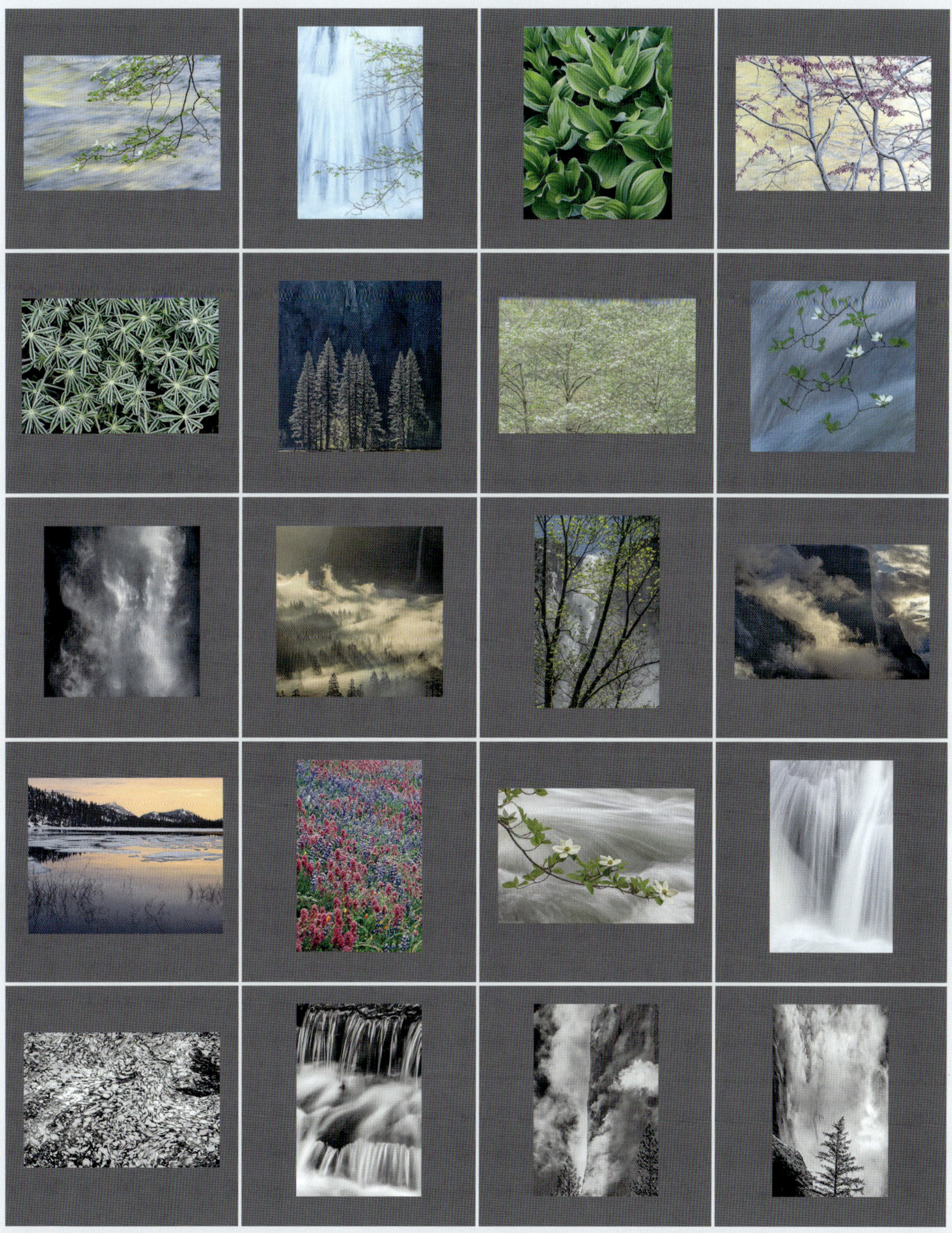

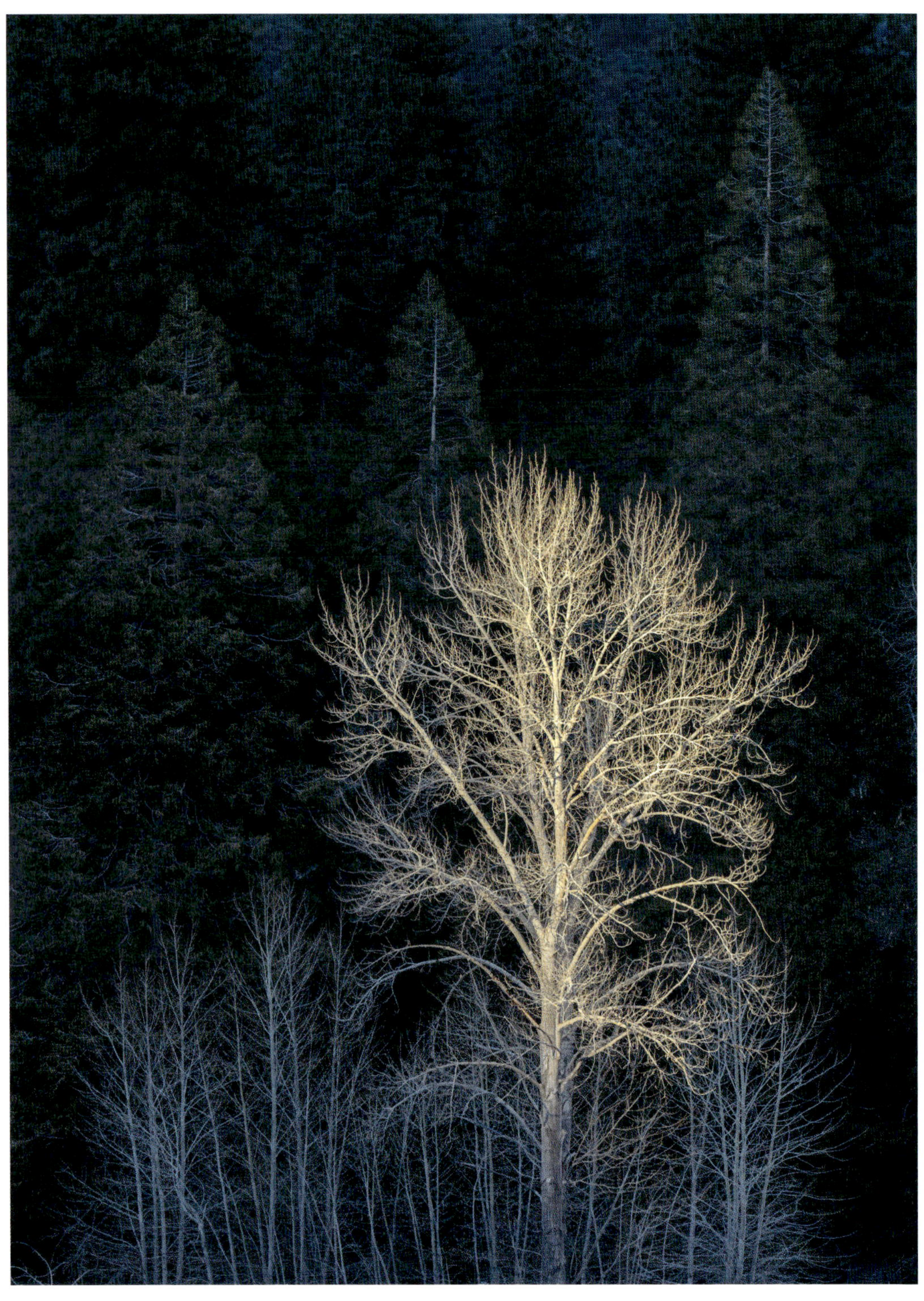

Last Light, Cottonwoods, Yosemite National Park, California, 2022

REFINE YOUR THEME

OVERVIEW

The objective of Lesson Six is to continue to photograph for and refine your theme. With new work to add depth, you can expand your theme to thirty to forty images.

ASSIGNMENT

Choose one of your established portfolios and consider how you might improve it. Place up to thirty images on your chosen theme in your collection folder. If you feel that you have two possible themes, you can add a folder for a secondary theme. (The assignment is described in more detail on page 68.)

The cycle of the previous lessons should be paying off so that you see a well-balanced set of images showing the characteristics we've previously discussed, such as consistent quality and variety of scale, lighting, weather, and season.

Blending the old and the new is our task again in this lesson. But how do we know what images successfully complement an established portfolio of work? Here are my keys to success for improving your thematic portfolios.

- Trust your instincts—Pay attention to your instincts and trust them. Your instincts and your preferences define your perspective. Follow new directions that pop into your head as you photograph or edit. Analyze later!

- Define and refine your theme, and have passion for it—As you photograph, and as you curate, keep refining your theme, and be open to redefining it if necessary. Ask yourself what the photos have to say.

- Maintain focused attention on the theme—Plan your photo sessions where you can best add to your topic.

Expect to work on the theme after this course, in locales with high potential, to give the project a chance to develop depth.

DEVELOPING DEPTH

Having a lot of outstanding photographs is always a good thing! A large, high-quality set of images gives you more options for presentations and/or marketing when it comes to portfolios. If you were to print some of your portfolio images as a small set of note cards, four or five photographs are enough. What if someone sees your note cards and asks you to hang an exhibit? Will you have twenty or thirty equally strong images? What if a book publisher sees your show and wants to print a book using 100 of your photographs? Isn't dreaming of such opportunities great motivation to get out there to photograph?

Another advantage of having an extensive body of work is that spin-off ideas for new themes are likely.

STORIES TO TELL

We all have stories to tell with our photographs. Sometimes the stories are about where we live or where we have been. Sometimes stories reveal the photographer's experiences unseen in the image

that, when heard, make the photograph all the more special. Your stories, about your life, about who you love, or about a place with which you connect deeply, are likely the best source for themes because they often reveal what is most important to you. Your most deeply felt and seen images will reach people's hearts!

We all have stories to tell with our photographs. Think about what stories you repeatedly tell with excitement. If you like to write, try writing short essays to go with your portfolio. At least consider taking notes, perhaps before or just after creating new images. Write down single words that describe emotions or moods you feel about the place or about the kind of images you wish to make or just made. When you refer back to your notes, words like "peaceful" or "energizing" may trigger ideas for a portfolio or a title or essay to go with it. Try creating photographs to fit the words.

With stories and images combined, you can powerfully convey a message, be it only how much fun you had on a photo tour, or more seriously, why you think a wild corner of your state should be preserved. If you are serious about promoting your photography, develop your writing or lecturing skills to better tell your stories.

On the opposite page is a group of images I made in and around my home. It has been difficult for me to make time to photograph over the last several years, so I've set out to create a new body of photographs I call "Home/Work." I have photographed still-life nature details in my home, and continue my nature studies by photographing the landscape around my home.

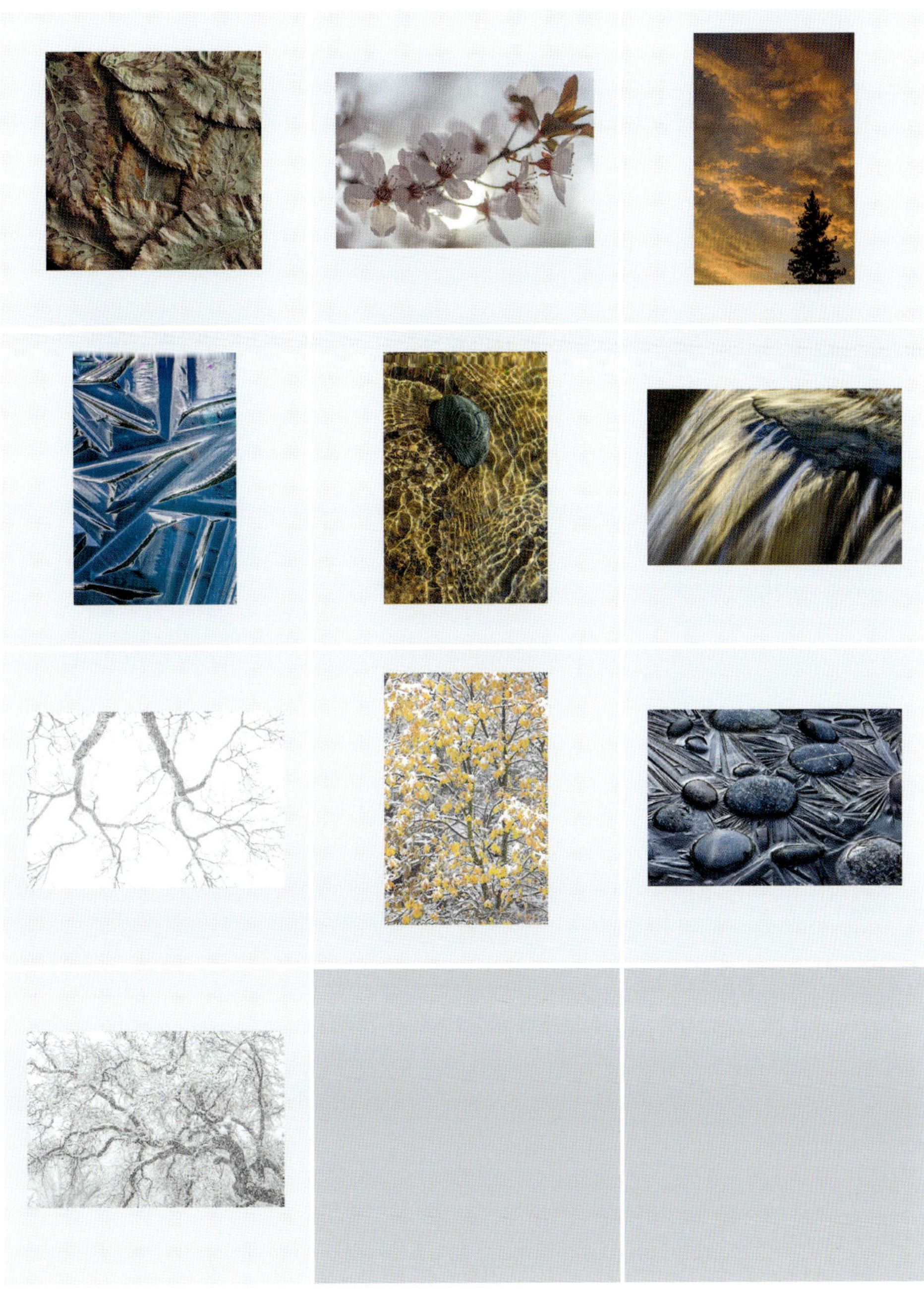

For this portfolio, I don't have to go on an expedition to make images, but I am able to keep my creative juices flowing. Most importantly, I have been very excited about the particular subjects I have been finding for this project. The images are diverse but united visually by the theme of nature and pattern. The portfolio title plays off the fact that I work at home and that my work blends with, and blurs into, my family life on a daily basis.

YOUR ASSIGNMENT: REFINE YOUR THEME

Choose one of your established portfolios and consider how you might improve it. If in your assessment of your images, you find them too similar, ask yourself what other subjects or approaches might add depth to your theme. Do you need more details? More portraits? A new location? Different light? In other words, what's missing?

Continue to refine your theme ideas, searching for just the right balance. For example, if I were to make a portfolio of my "Home/Work" group on the previous page, how well do my sharp and literal images blend together with my impressionistic work? For me, it depends on the context, editing with a specific project in mind. For a fine art portfolio, I would keep the abstracts to themselves. If a nature magazine wanted to publish a photo-essay on lupine, I would submit both descriptive and more artsy photographs.

Photograph or research your archives specifically with the needs of the portfolio in mind. Plan your photo sessions for this assignment in terms of location, subject, time of day, etc., with these needs in mind to maximize your time.

Refer back to the suggestions I offered in the assignment for Lesson Five (page 60)—they apply just as much with this lesson. The practice, the repetition of the feedback loop, can be used on any theme and with future projects. Many of my themes are lifelong projects that I have developed over decades, and I plan on continuing to develop them into the future.

Place up to thirty images on your chosen theme in your Lesson Six Collection folder. If you feel that you have two possible themes, you can add a folder for a secondary theme. However, for the final assignment in Lesson Eight, I will be asking you to create a final, completed portfolio. This is a good time to get feedback on and refine your main theme, whether that is through self-assessment or a mentor or friend.

YOSEMITE PORTFOLIO CASE STUDY

For this example, I am selecting thirty photographs from Yosemite Valley. As most of my favorite images for the book will be from there, this is a good opportunity to collect them to see what I have, and what I might add when I go into the final selection for the book. I have a target total of photographs I want for the final selection of 100–130 images. In my experience, any editing process involves many rounds of refinement.

This example should give you an idea of how I view and assess a collection of finalists for the book. It is hard to put into words what works for me with these photographs, but in general, I have used the following criteria:

- Intimate landscapes

- Fresh viewpoints, less published images

- Few icons

- Yosemite and surrounding environs

You might work on establishing a list of criteria specific to your given theme. The more you go through this type of analysis, the better you can sense whether the selected images convey the criteria. To create this selection, it took me three to four rounds of analyzing the individual images, where I thought I had it right, took a break, and then came back to further rework the grouping. Be persistent, give yourself time to reevaluate, seek advice, and in the final analysis, trust your instincts.

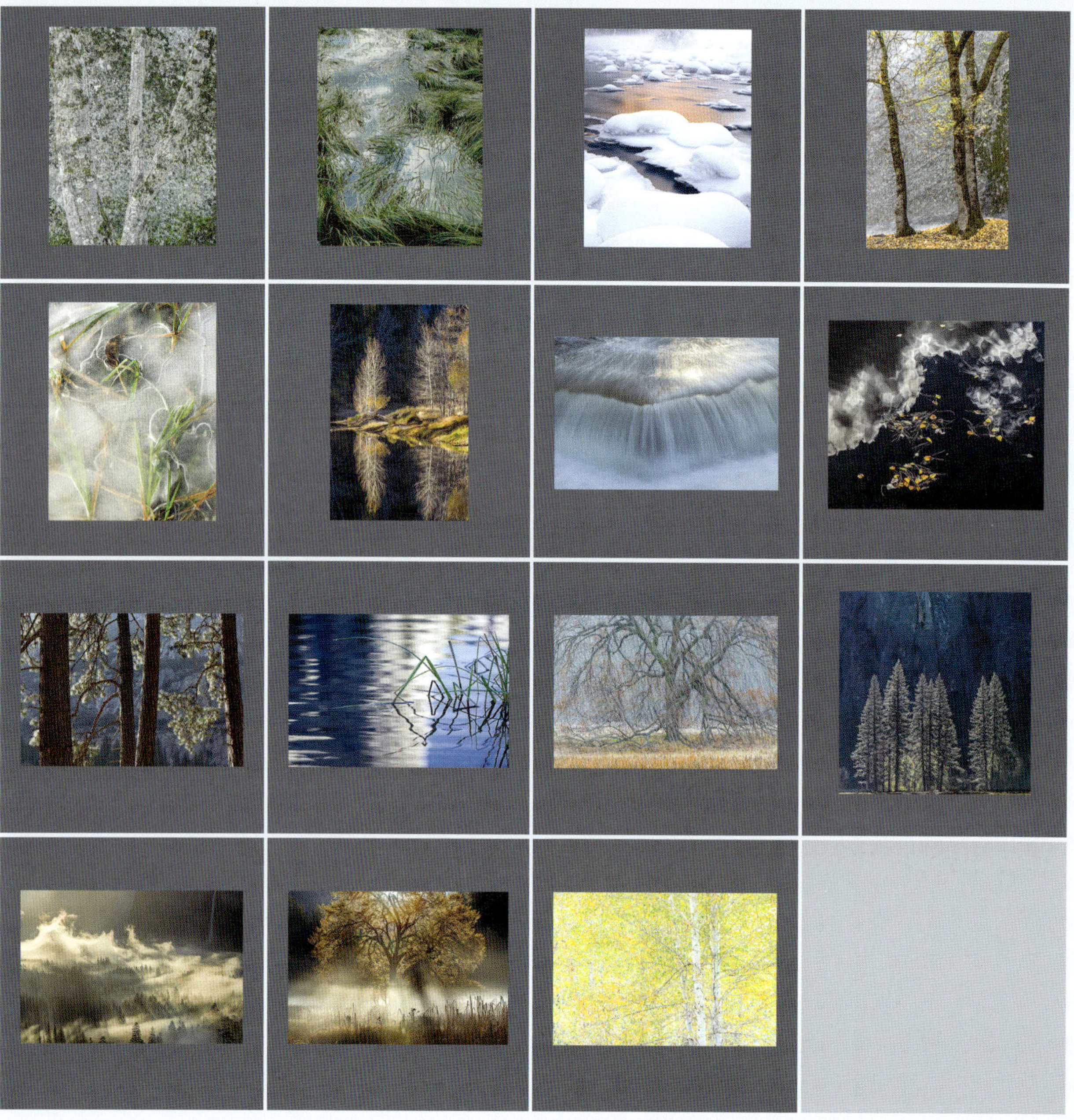

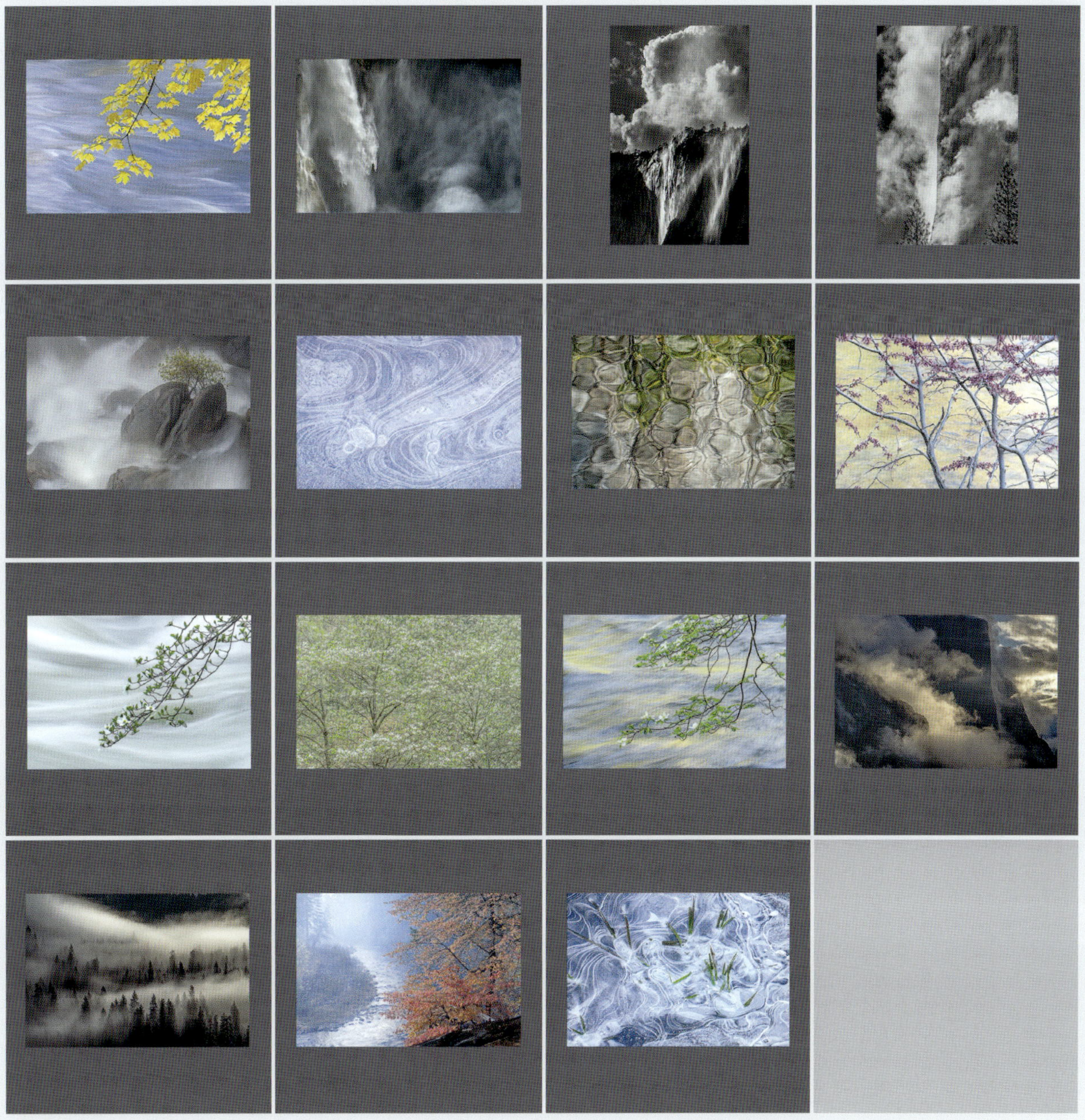

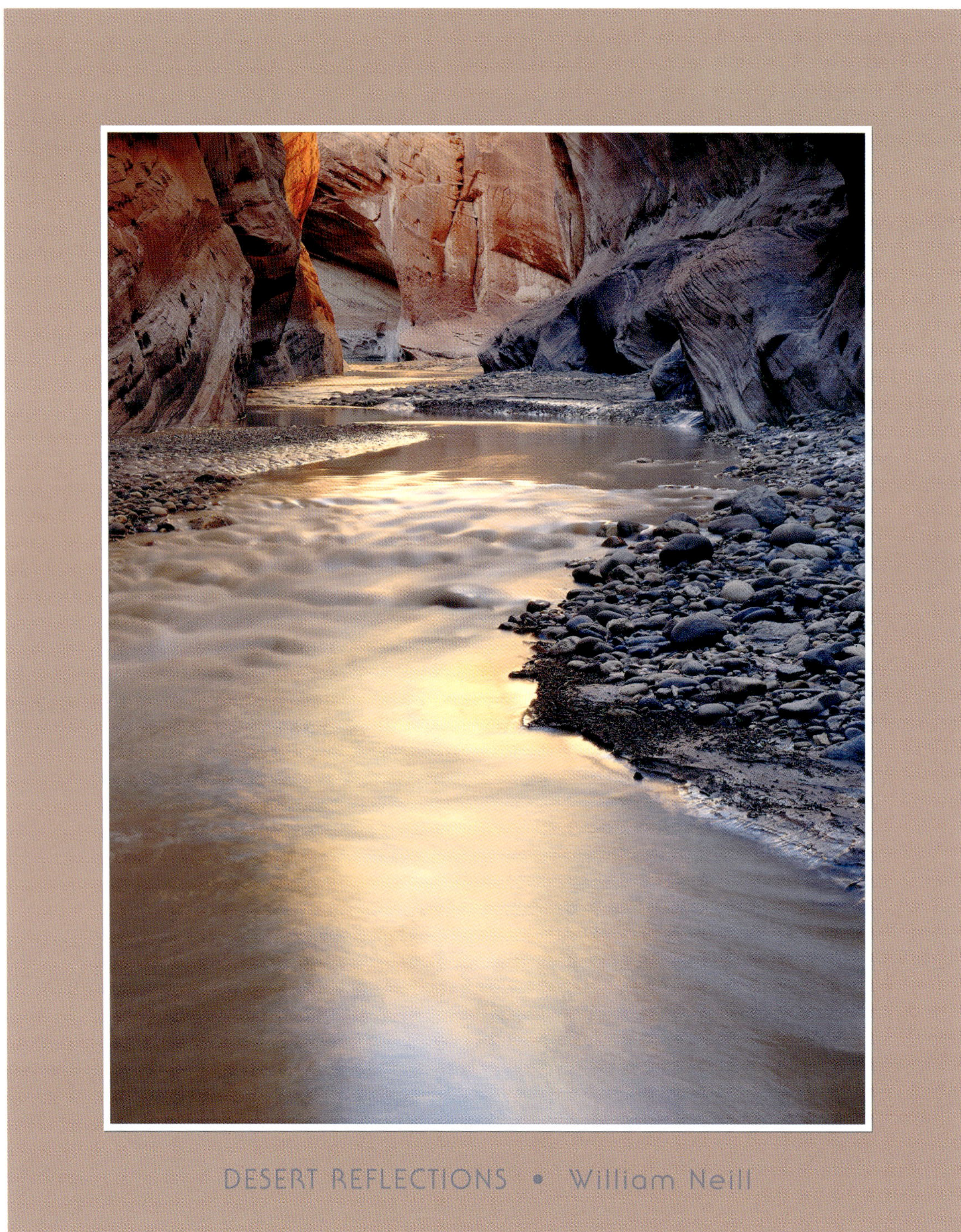

Reflections, Paria River Poster

LESSON 7

WHERE YOU CAN GO FROM HERE— IDEAS AND RESOURCES

OVERVIEW

The objective of Lesson Seven is to work on a specific presentation to practice the realization and presentation of your portfolio.

ASSIGNMENT

Choose the theme you wish to use for your final presentation. Add up to thirty images on this theme to your collection, including at least three new photos. (The assignment is described in more detail on page 86.)

Now that you have worked hard to build your portfolio, it is time to reap your rewards. There are few things as rewarding to a photographer as seeing an elegant presentation featuring one's own art. I will be practical in this lesson, list different types of presentations, and include links to facilitate learning more about your options. Choices include creating things like a book, a slideshow, or prints for an art show, exhibition, or your home.

Discovering what you want to do with your work is a fun and challenging process. Keeping in mind the previous lessons on curating your images into a beautiful portfolio, maintaining high quality and a consistent theme, you will find that whatever your chosen forms of presentation are, the results will have a more substantial impact than without applying these principles.

FINE ART PRINTS

For many photographers, the ultimate expression of their art is a high-quality photographic print. I have used many options for making the fine art prints I sell in galleries, from making Cibachrome prints in Ansel's darkroom in Yosemite to using high-end custom labs, to finally having my own professional-grade inkjet printer in my studio. I have Canon printers with which I make prints for my galleries and art consultants. I am currently using the Canon Pro-2100.

A lot of the fun of photography these days, especially digital photography, is the ease with which you can make excellent prints even with the less-expensive printers. Canon, HP, and Epson all make first-rate printers. Even if you have no interest in marketing your photographs, making a few prints for yourself, your family, or friends is a great reward for all your effort. Besides, if you wish to improve your skill in Photoshop or another digital imaging software, making a series of proof prints lets you see more clearly the results of adjustments made on the computer.

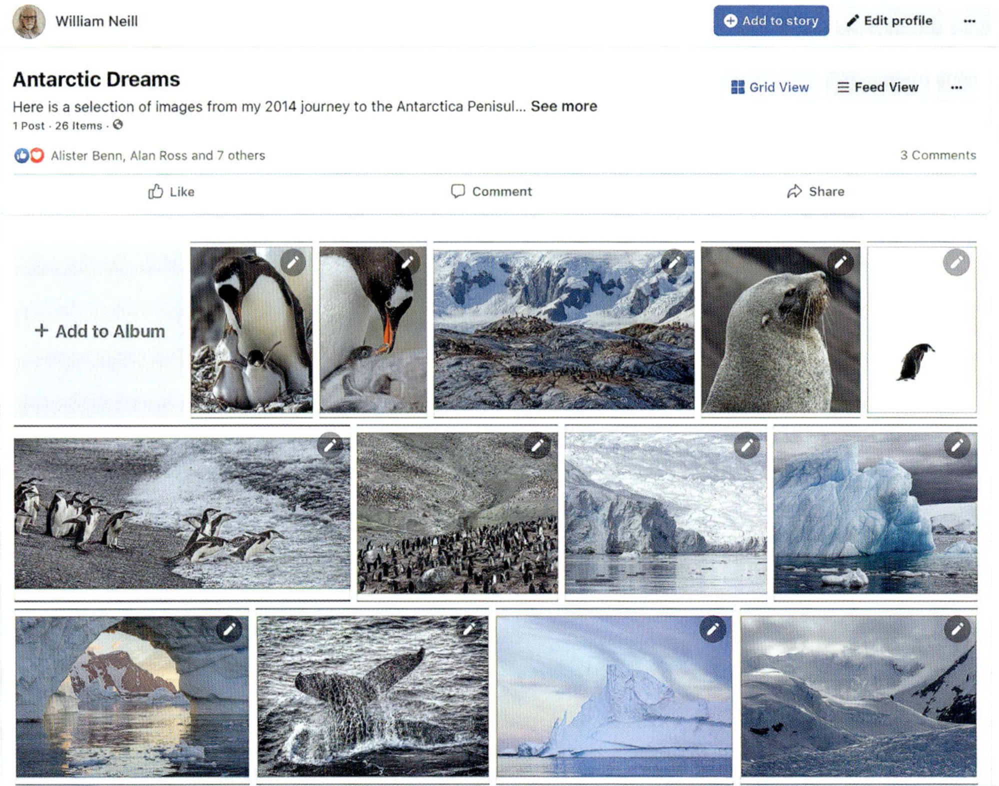

An album of my Antarctica photographs on my Facebook page.

Whether you make your own prints or use a custom lab, the matting and framing will formalize your imagery, making the whole process more rewarding, and communicating clearly to all that you are an artist.

SOCIAL MEDIA

It is very difficult to overestimate the impact that social media platforms (Facebook, Twitter, Instagram, Flickr, YouTube, etc.) have had on the world in general, and especially on photography. I joined the movement in the early years as a way to reach a broader audience, promote my business, stay relevant to younger audiences, and most importantly, to share my art. Social media pages serve as a pathway to our webpages where the full effect of our imagery can be featured.

I have found social media useful as a diary of my creative life, which helps me channel ideas for portfolios, books, and essays. When I write a blog post or magazine article, I often refer back to my posts to see what creative concepts I might discuss. I can spot trends in my images to expand upon, whether I'm writing an essay or making new photographs.

There are few things as rewarding to a photographer as seeing an elegant presentation featuring one's own art.

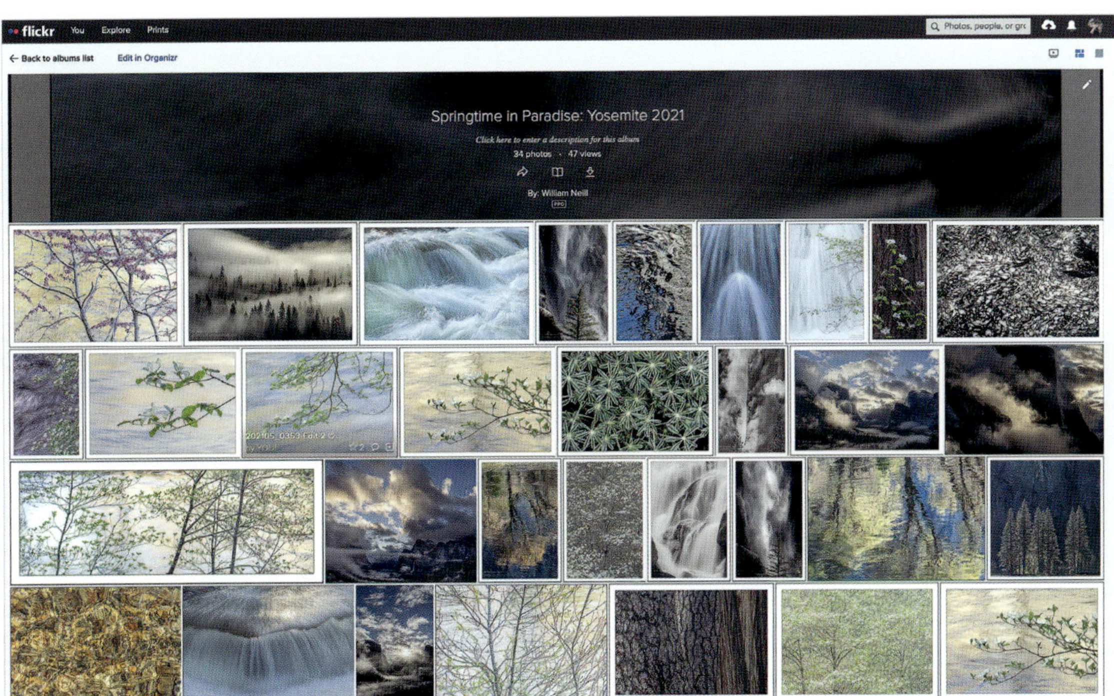

My Flickr album features new work made in the spring of 2021 in Yosemite.

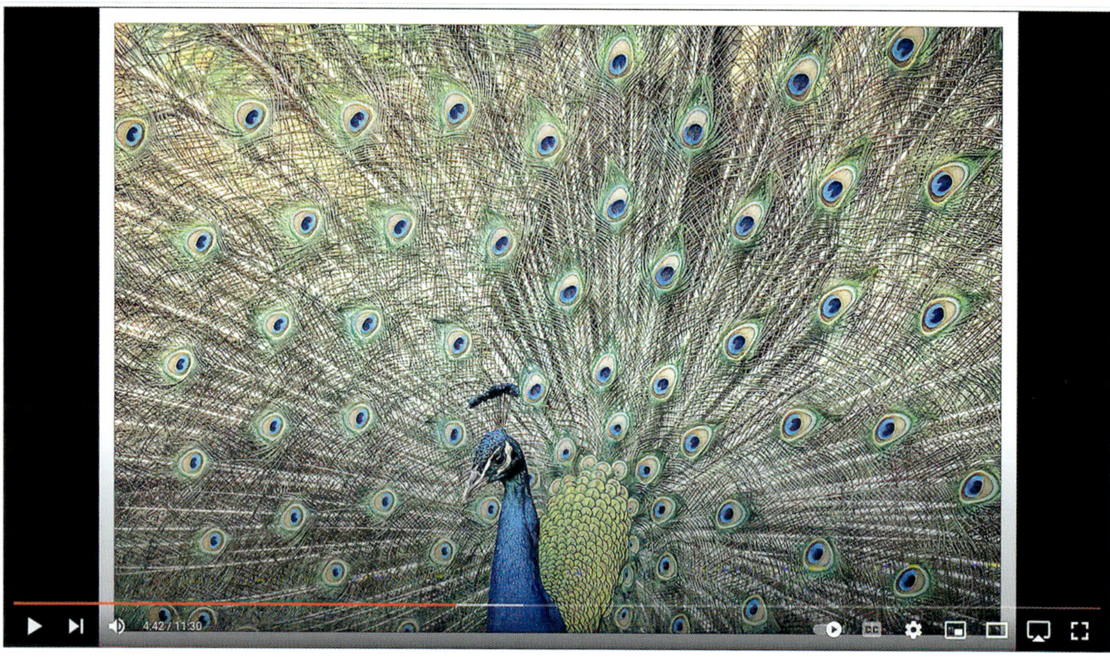

Favorite Photographs of 2020 by William Neill

On my YouTube page, I created a video slideshow of my favorite images from 2020.

There are many ways to make social media work for you, but I recommend not becoming too attached to the number of followers or likes you receive. If you don't already have an internal mindset about listening to your artistic instincts, you can end up letting outside response to your images become the driving force for your creative output, rather than being guided by your heart and vision. I don't pretend to not notice which of my images are more popular on social media, or not to like the attention some images receive. But I developed as an artist long before I began using social media, and I won't let it dictate what or how I photograph.

NFTS

Non-fungible tokens (NFTs) are a method to sell unique digital images using new blockchain and cryptocurrency technologies. Photographers and other artists can "mint" their digital images and collections on cloud platforms and sell them through cryptocurrency marketplaces. NFTs offer a new opportunity and channel for photographers to generate income for their livelihoods. In terms of portfolio development, NFTs are often released in thematic collections with an artist's statement that gives the potential buyer insight into how and why they create their art.

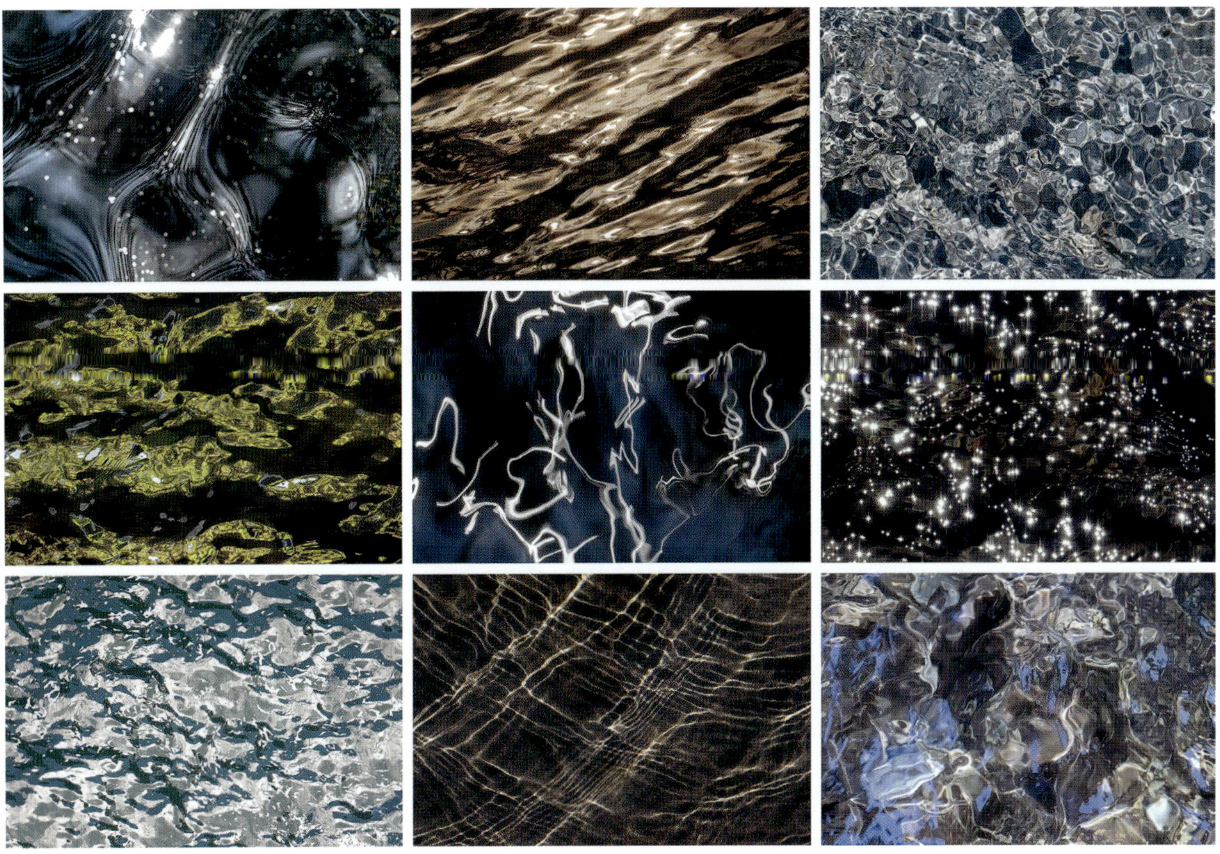

Here is a sample collection by photographer TJ Thorne from his Twitter feed, featuring his "Ebb and Flow" collection of NFTs for sale on OpenSea, a major marketplace for NFTs.

"With images spanning a period of six years, Ebb and Flow is a collection of 100 images that tell the story of my search for serenity through the act of photographing water. These images are as close to my heart that my photography gets and is one of the most personally meaningful things I've ever created." —TJ Thorne

WEB GALLERIES AND BLOGS

Most photographers will have a webpage where they upload portfolios of their images. In many cases, you can upload a gallery on a given theme and include a store option for purchasing. I use PhotoShelter for my main webpage and Wordpress for my blog. There are many options provided by PhotoShelter, including: websites, cloud storage & organization, client proofing & delivery, e-commerce, and marketing tools.

Each hosting option has its pros and cons, but most, like PhotoShelter, offer e-commerce and print fulfillment, the ability to create multiple portfolio galleries for all of your themes, and client sharing through review, selection, and purchases. Each company offers a variety of page layout templates to choose from so you can give your site the look you prefer. PhotoShelter has the advantage of working with WordPress to incorporate a blog within its pages. Its cloud storage serves as a backup option for high-resolution files. When you are ready to build a new website, research your options carefully, as features and pricing might change. Some services include:

- **PhotoShelter** https://www.photoshelter.com

- **SmugMug** https://www.smugmug.com

- **Squarespace** https://www.squarespace.com

- **Zenfolio** https://zenfolio.com

- **WordPress** https://wordpress.com

DIGITAL PRESENTATIONS

Suppose you are asked to present your photography to a local photography group, such as a camera club, environmental group, or at a photography workshop. In this situation, you'll need to learn how to make a professional-quality lecture from your images. Here are a few options for software you can use to create presentations:

- Adobe Lightroom

- Acrobat

- Keynote (Mac)

- PowerPoint

ONLINE BOOK PRINTERS

Along with the growth of Internet commerce, photographers now have a number of options for printing books. The quality of books is very good, and the options (such as size, page layout, paper quality options, cover stock, etc.) are expanding as demand increases. I've used Lightroom's Book module to make a book layout, which can be sent directly to Blurb for printing from within Lightroom.

For my *Antarctic Dreams* book/eBook, I used Lightroom's Book layout options, where the images you put into a Collections theme is sent to the Book module. Once you make your image selection in the Library module and set up a page layout template, the Auto Layout function puts your book together. In the Book module, you can visualize the details of the design, such as the border size, sequencing and pairing of images, and caption font and size. You can easily move photos around to improve the sequencing or drop images that don't contribute in terms of quality or context. If you save your settings, you can create new books with the same design.

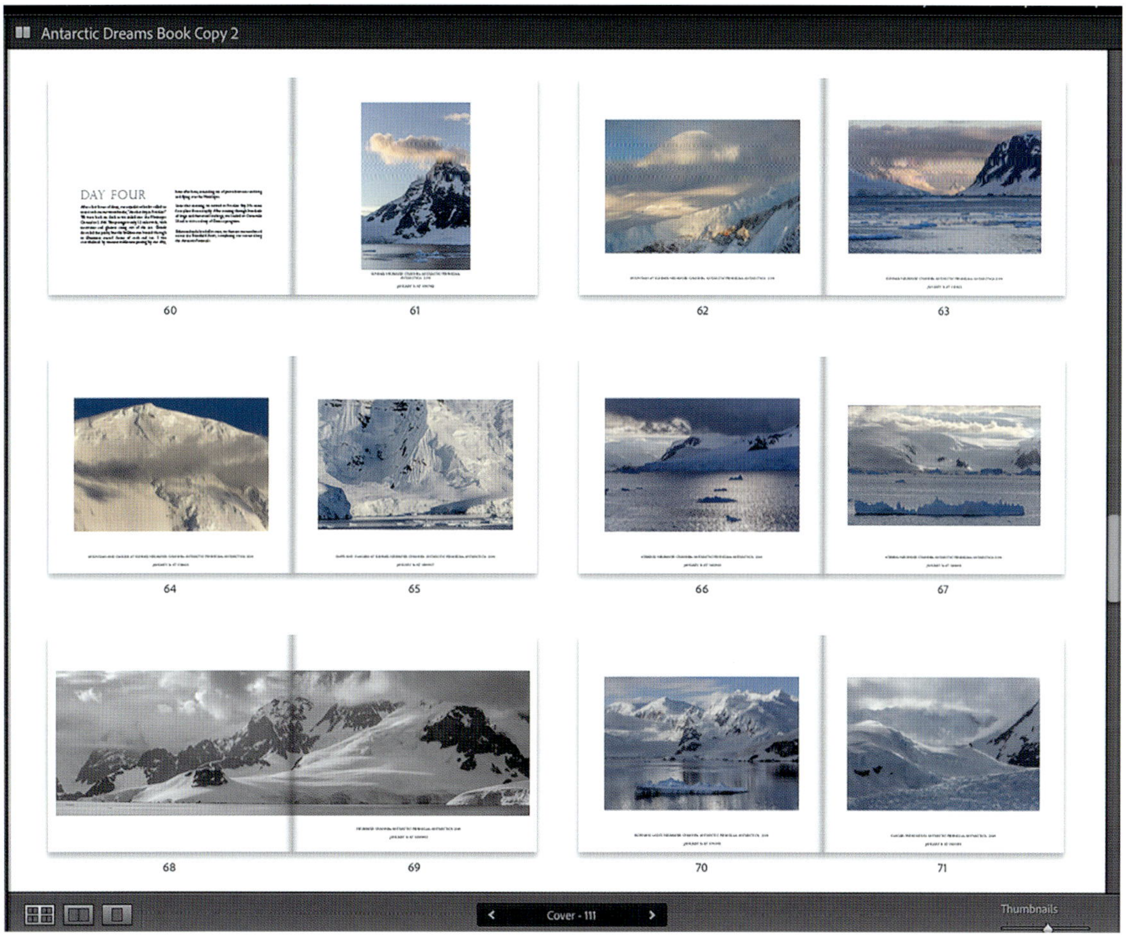

Blurb

Blurb (www.blurb.com) provides options for printing hard copies of your book as well as for eBook creation and sales. They also offer options for photo books, wall art, trade books, magazines, and notebooks. You can then choose from a number of distribution options, including the Blurb Bookstore, Amazon, Ingram, Apple iBooks Store, and even Kickstarter.

MagCloud

Another service that provides many output options is MagCloud (www.magcloud.com), which is owned by Blurb but is more focused on business and promotional needs. They offer magazine, pamphlet, square, and tabloid publications, as well as flyers, posters, and digital options.

SELF-PRINTABLE BOOKS

If you have an inkjet printer, one exciting way to present your images is to print a book yourself. In this case, you are in control of the design and quality of output. These books can be offered for sale, given as gifts, or presented to potential customers as a catalog for print sales. The quality of the printing should very closely match that of your fine art prints. Your custom book can be designed—with text for captions, essays, and page numbers—using page layout software such as Adobe InDesign.

Most major inkjet paper manufacturers make double-sided paper for making books and portfolios. Canson, Hahnemühle, Moab, Red River, and Ilford are among the brands that offer double-sided inkjet papers. There are many binding options available for handmade books. Moab and Hahnemühle have offered packages that include inkjet paper and a book cover into which the printed pages are placed.

PHOTOGRAPHY COMPETITIONS

Competitions offer you a chance to test your best photos against other photographers. Many contests have a major Photographer or Photograph of the Year award, but they also have subcategories that are more specialized in terms of a specific style or genre within the competition.

I entered the Communication Arts Photography Awards annual competition early in my career and received their Award of Excellence five different years. The connection with their editor lead to a feature article, which then lead to stock sales and a major poster-publishing contract. You never know

who will see your photographs, and good things can happen, as they did for me. Your editing skill will be critical in showing only your best work.

Success in competitions can include cash and equipment prizes, as well as opportunities for interviews for magazines, on podcasts, or with YouTube channels that discuss your type of photography. In general, more exposure is a good thing!

> CAVEAT: Some contests will claim the copyright to winning images. For example, camera manufacturers sponsor contests, often with the ethically questionable catch that they can use a winning picture in advertising, free to them. My advice is to check competition guidelines carefully, and do NOT give away your copyright to anyone.

National Geographic Photography Competitions
https://www.nationalgeographic.com/contests

National Geographic Photography Competitions are one of the most popular and prestigious contests in the world. Major categories include Nature, Travel, and Landscape photography.

International Photography Awards
https://www.photoawards.com/

The IPA mission is "to salute the achievements of the world's finest photographers, to discover new and emerging talent, and to promote the appreciation of photography." Thirteen different categories cover a wide range of genres including Advertising, Architecture, Editorial, People, Nature, and Sports.

Smithsonian Photo Contest

https://photocontest.smithsonianmag.com/
photocontest/

Categories include Natural World, People, Travel, The American Experience, Altered Images, and Mobile.

Hasselblad Master Awards

https://www.hasselblad.com/inspiration/

This competition is one of the world's most prestigious professional photographic competitions, with a full range of categories.

Wildlife Photographer of the Year

https://www.nhm.ac.uk/wpy/

Wildlife Photographer of the Year uses photography to celebrate the diversity of life, and inspire, inform, and create advocates for our planet. The competition is well known for championing ethical wildlife photography, rewarding truthful representations of nature that display respect for animals and the environment. The contest has a wide variety of categories. Single-image categories include Animals in their Environment, Animal Portraits, Behaviour: Amphibians and Reptiles, Behaviour: Birds, Behaviour: Invertebrates, Behaviour: Mammals, Oceans—The Bigger Picture, Plants and Fungi, Natural Artistry, Underwater, Urban Wildlife, Wetlands—The Bigger Picture, and Photojournalism.

International Landscape Photographer of the Year Awards

https://www.internationallandscapephotographer.com/index.php

Categories include Monochrome, Aerial, Snow and Ice, Night Sky, and Urban Environment.

Landscape Photographer of the Year

https://www.lpoty.co.uk

Categories include Classic View, Urban Life, Your View, and Black and White.

Natural Landscape Photography Awards

https://naturallandscapeawards.com

A competition for those landscape photographers who dedicate themselves to capturing the beauty of the landscape in a realistic manner. Categories include Natural Landscape Photographer of the Year, Photograph of the Year, Youth Photographer of the Year, Grand Landscape, Intimate & Abstract Award, Nightscape, Aerial, and Projects.

Communication Arts Photography Competition

https://www.commarts.com/
competition/2022-photography

CA's Award of Excellence is one of the most-coveted awards in the industry. Communication Arts is the largest international trade journal of visual communications covering graphic design, advertising, photography, illustration, and interactive media.

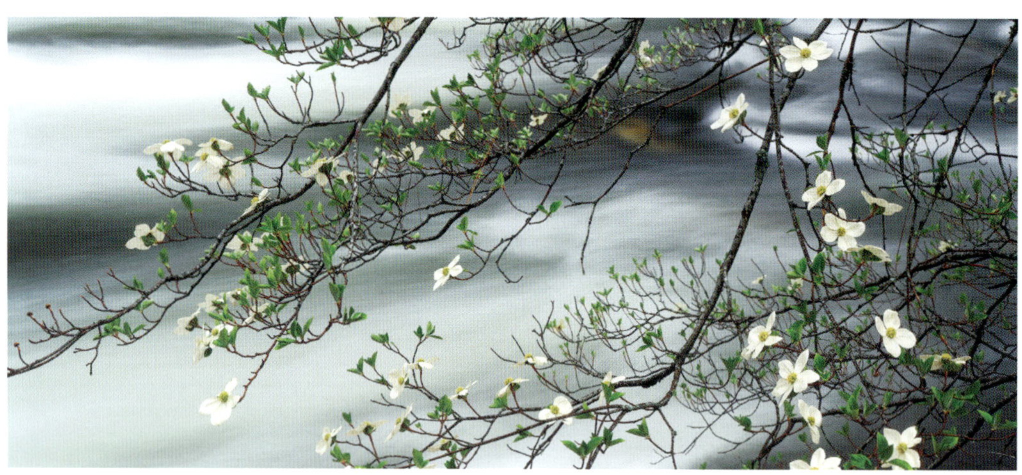

WILLIAM NEILL | DOGWOOD AND MERCED RIVER, YOSEMITE NATIONAL PARK

POSTERS

The modern inkjet printer offers tremendous flexibility for small-scale publishing, allowing you to design your layout and print on demand for presentations or sales. If you don't have your own printer, some labs will offer poster printing with volume discounts. If you design and prepare the file for the printer, you can order a print that includes your graphics, at your custom size. If you already have or are establishing a market for your photography, such as art fairs, this will give your customers a less expensive option. Remember, you can always print just one!

If your self-published posters sell well, you might develop a market and find a publisher for them. I have had an extensive history in poster publishing, with worldwide distribution through major publishers and also by self-publishing.

The image above is a mock-up design I made in Photoshop to show my poster publisher how the photographs might look if they were published. The same files can easily be sent to any photo lab for output, usually on less expensive paper than high-quality inkjet media.

PORTFOLIO BINDERS

I have used high-quality binders for many types of presentations over the years. On the following page are some sample pages that, when assembled in a binder, I leave with galleries for display or send to art consultants for presentations. Binder portfolios are a great way to show many images at once, and the binders are easy to update. The binders work especially well if they are printed on the same material as your final prints so that viewers can see the quality they can expect if they purchase a photograph. Since the pages are removable, the images within can be updated easily over time.

Prat (www.prat-usa.com/index.html) is a reliable company that offers high-quality portfolio display products.

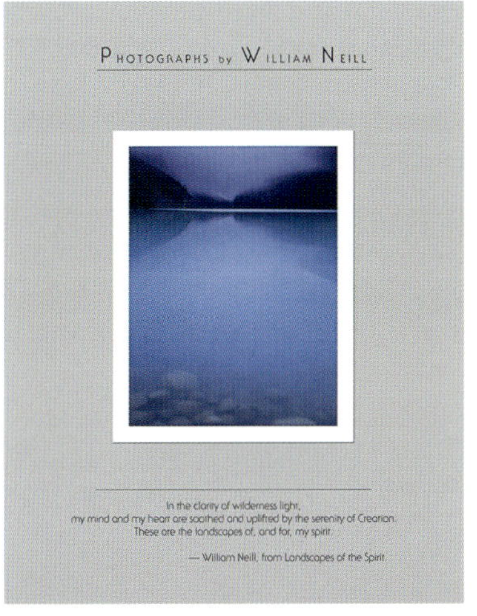

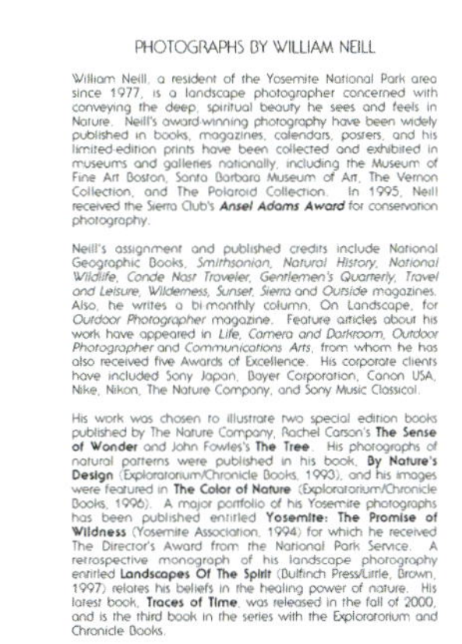

PHOTOGRAPHS BY WILLIAM NEILL

William Neill, a resident of the Yosemite National Park area since 1977, is a landscape photographer concerned with conveying the deep, spiritual beauty he sees and feels in Nature. Neill's award-winning photography have been widely published in books, magazines, calendars, posters, and his limited-edition prints have been collected and exhibited in museums and galleries nationally, including the Museum of Fine Art Boston, Santa Barbara Museum of Art, The Vernon Collection, and The Polaroid Collection. In 1995, Neill received the Sierra Club's **Ansel Adams Award** for conservation photography.

Neill's assignment and published credits include National Geographic Books, Smithsonian, Natural History, National Wildlife, Condé Nast Traveler, Gentlemen's Quarterly, Travel and Leisure, Wilderness, Sunset, Sierra and Outside magazines. Also, he writes a bi-monthly column, On Landscape, for Outdoor Photographer magazine. Feature articles about his work have appeared in Life, Camera and Darkroom, Outdoor Photographer and Communications Arts, from whom he has also received five Awards of Excellence. His corporate clients have included Sony Japan, Bayer Corporation, Canon USA, Nike, Nikon, The Nature Company, and Sony Music Classical.

His work was chosen to illustrate two special edition books published by The Nature Company, Rachel Carson's **The Sense of Wonder** and John Fowles's **The Tree**. His photographs of natural patterns were published in his book, **By Nature's Design** (Exploratorium/Chronicle Books, 1993), and his images were featured in **The Color of Nature** (Exploratorium/Chronicle Books, 1996). A major portfolio of his Yosemite photographs has been published entitled **Yosemite: The Promise of Wildness** (Yosemite Association, 1994) for which he received The Director's Award from the National Park Service. A retrospective monograph of his landscape photography entitled **Landscapes Of The Spirit** (Bulfinch Press/Little, Brown, 1997) relates his beliefs in the healing power of nature. His latest book, **Traces of Time**, was released in the fall of 2000, and is the third book in the series with the Exploratorium and Chronicle Books.

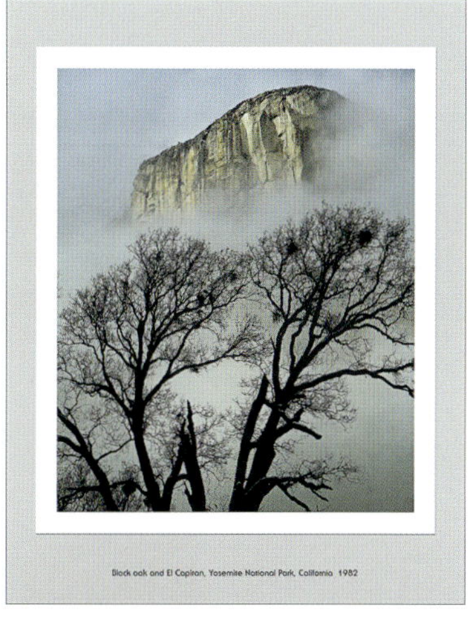

Black oak and El Capitan, Yosemite National Park, California 1982

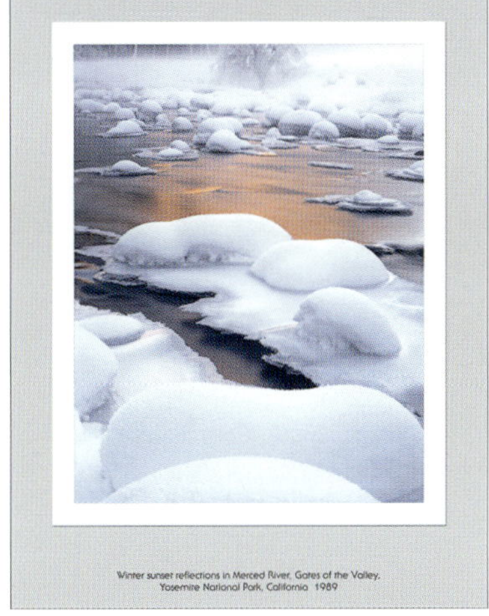

In the clarity of wilderness light,
my mind and my heart are soothed and uplifted by the serenity of Creation.
These are the landscapes of, and for, my spirit.

— William Neill, from Landscapes of the Spirit.

Winter sunset reflections in Merced River, Gates of the Valley,
Yosemite National Park, California 1989

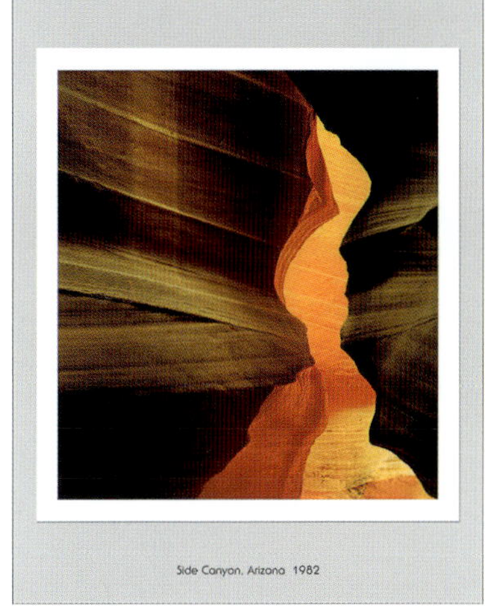

Side Canyon, Arizona 1982

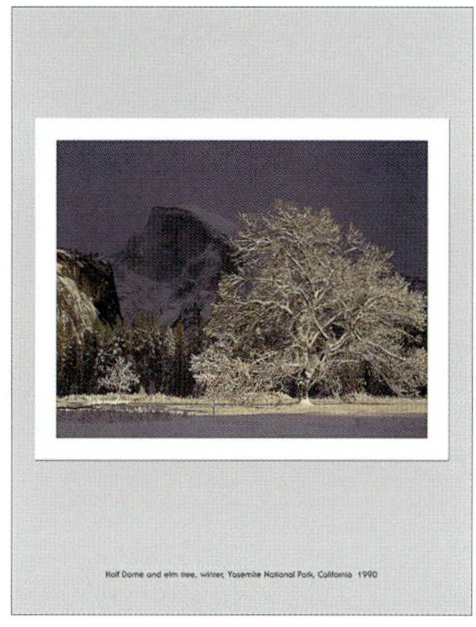

Half Dome and elm tree, winter, Yosemite National Park, California 1990

IMPORTANT NOTE:

Archive Your Images I strongly suggest making a habit of backing up all of your digital image files—on CDs or DVDs, on secondary hard drives, or via a cloud service. I use BackBlaze (https://www.backblaze.com), which backs up my files to their cloud continuously when my computers are on. I also store hard drive backups in my safe deposit box at my local bank.

THE IMPORTANCE OF GRAPHIC DESIGN

In this chapter, I have shown examples of various output options for your photography, such as posters, books, and portfolio pages, to not only illustrate the product options, but also show the graphic design quality. Photographers invest in improving their photography by buying books, learning processing techniques, and taking workshops. When you achieve a high level in your imagery, the design quality of your presentation needs to match. When I've taught my portfolio development course online, I've often seen the graphic quality bring down a portfolio presentation.

One common problem photographers run into is type issues, such as using too large or heavy of a type, thus causing the text to compete with the photographs. Another common issue is placing too many images on a page and not allowing enough space around each image.

When it comes to designing your own layout, modern software makes it easy for folks to think they can design at a professional level. I suggest that you

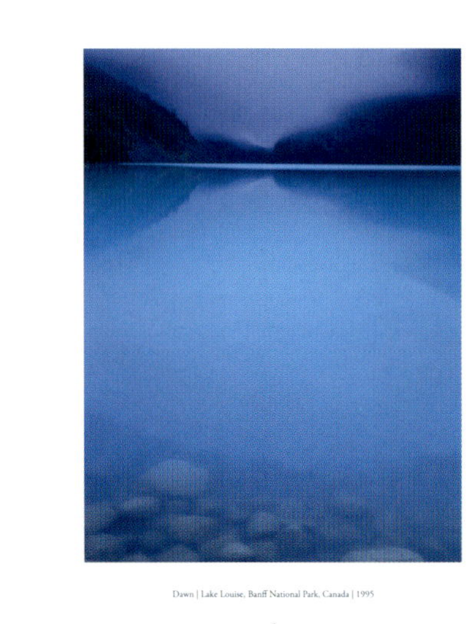

Here are several page spreads from my recent book *Light on the Landscape* that illustrate to me clean graphic design with plenty of space around the images, and type that doesn't draw away from the photographs (above and opposite page).

study the graphic design of books or websites that appeal to you, or maybe even take a graphic design course. Learning how to use design software such as Adobe's InDesign will be important if you plan to lay out a book yourself. When I make the final layout for my Yosemite book, InDesign will be my software of choice, but my modest skills will be tested.

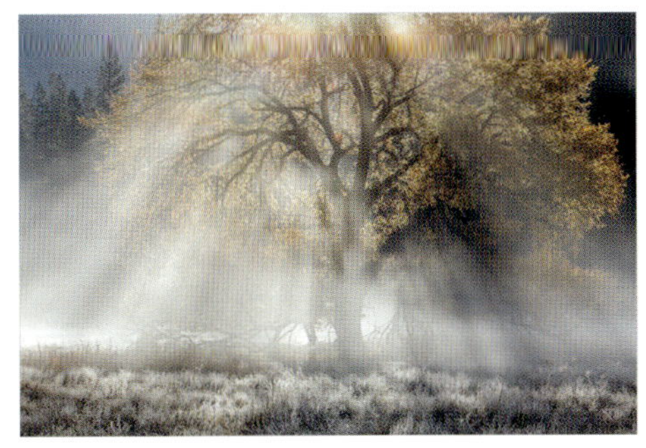

Autumn Elm and Sunbeams | Cook's Meadow, Yosemite National Park, California | 2014

94

FOCUS YOUR FALL PORTFOLIO

WORK WITH A THEME TO CREATE A UNIQUE COLLECTION OF IMAGES

When autumn photography season approaches, I start to anticipate making new photographs. I have some ideas to share that may help you develop an excellent portfolio for the fall season. I have found it useful, for myself and for teaching my students, to think about creating a story line, or clear thematic focus. Consider what specific locations or aspects of autumn inspire you the most. The location could be your backyard, a nearby park or reserve, or a travel location where you can spend at least a few days to explore the area fully. A favorite aspect might include colorful reflections or the patterns of fallen leaves. This approach of specialization will help distinguish your autumn images from other photographers' work.

Two key elements needed for your selection of an autumn theme are passion for the subject and easy access during the season. Passion is a must-have ingredient for creative, insightful imagery. Repeated

95

Light on the Landscape

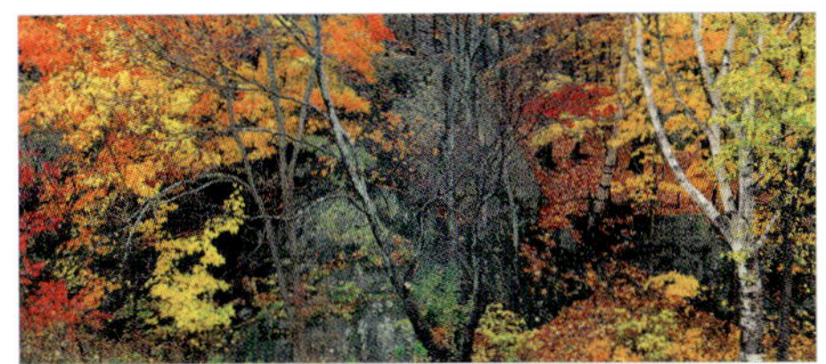

Autumn Forest | Baxter State Park, Maine | 1995

I made full-framed exposures as well as panoramic ones like this one. Although pleased with both, I especially liked how the rhythm of color and design is portrayed in the narrow format. The key quality in this photograph for me is the soft lighting provided by the rainstorm. That the leaves were wet and many of them had fallen to the forest floor adds impact to the image. The hanging and fallen leaves blend somewhat in the composition, and this ambiguity gives the viewer pause to look more closely.

Another favorite lighting condition for me is backlighting. When light comes from behind colorful leaves, the glow can be magical. The best times to find good backlight are early morning or late afternoon when the sun is low in the sky. Although aiming your camera toward the sun can be a challenge, you can get great results with a little extra care. Lens flare can be a problem, so watch for that in the viewfinder. When inside the forest, the simplest solution for flare is to use tree shadows to block the sun. The trees can become strongly silhouetted, the leaves brilliant, and the issue of flare eliminated.

The photograph *Kings Pond with Morning Mist* was made at sunrise. My wife and I drove off from our motel in predawn darkness into the Green Mountains, hoping for great light and autumn color at

98

Focus Your Fall Portfolio

this pond we had spotted the day before. In spite of the fact that I had no clue exactly when sunrise was or where the sun would rise, a little luck goes a long way. A nighttime rainstorm was just clearing at dawn, and the fog lifted to reveal this glorious scene.

The wide scope of this scene required my 90mm lens (about 24mm focal length on a 35mm full-frame format) on my 4x5 camera. I aimed the camera just far enough away from the sun to avoid direct sunlight, shaded my lens carefully, and photographed quickly in the rapidly changing light.

When you plan your next autumn's field sessions, think about the lighting conditions and about what thematic project you could develop or add to. Think about what you want to say with your images. Your unique viewpoint will be better revealed, and the concept behind the photographs will heighten your portfolio's impact.

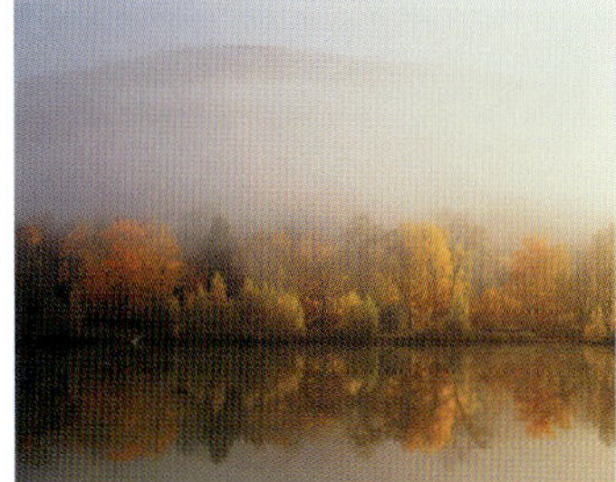

Kings Pond with Morning Mist | Green Mountain National Forest, Vermont | 1991

99

For many, learning design software with the complexity of a program like Photoshop will be more work than it's worth, especially for a book. Seek help by asking other photographers if they know of any designers they would recommend consulting with or hiring to design your project. As discussed earlier in this chapter, book printers such as Blurb offer many templates for book layouts, and I've found Lightroom's Book module to be very useful. But whatever choice you make for creating a book, your choice of type, borders, and sequencing will be critical.

For a simple, one-page item such as a poster, I've found that Photoshop works very well with its type, color picker, and layers tools.

Personal tastes will vary, but the more you learn about clean graphic design, the better your output will be.

YOUR ASSIGNMENT: PREPARE FOR YOUR FINAL PORTFOLIO

I suggest that you continue to photograph and add new images to one of your established themes. When working on your presentation concept, you may need more photographs for that context and form of presentation, so think about what else the group requires and make one last effort to add more depth to your collection of images.

Now is the time to select your final portfolio theme. Choose the theme you wish to use for your final presentation, which will be used for your final assignment in Lesson Eight. Add up to thirty images on this theme to your Lesson Seven Collection folder, including at least three new photos.

Continue to refine your artist's statement for your selected theme.

YOSEMITE PORTFOLIO CASE STUDY

For my upcoming Yosemite book, I am using an existing InDesign document as my template. At the time of writing, I am in the preliminary stages of image selection and design for the Yosemite book.

Until I make my final selections and take them to InDesign, I am using Lightroom to visualize my choices, and also to show you how you can do the same for your book ideas.

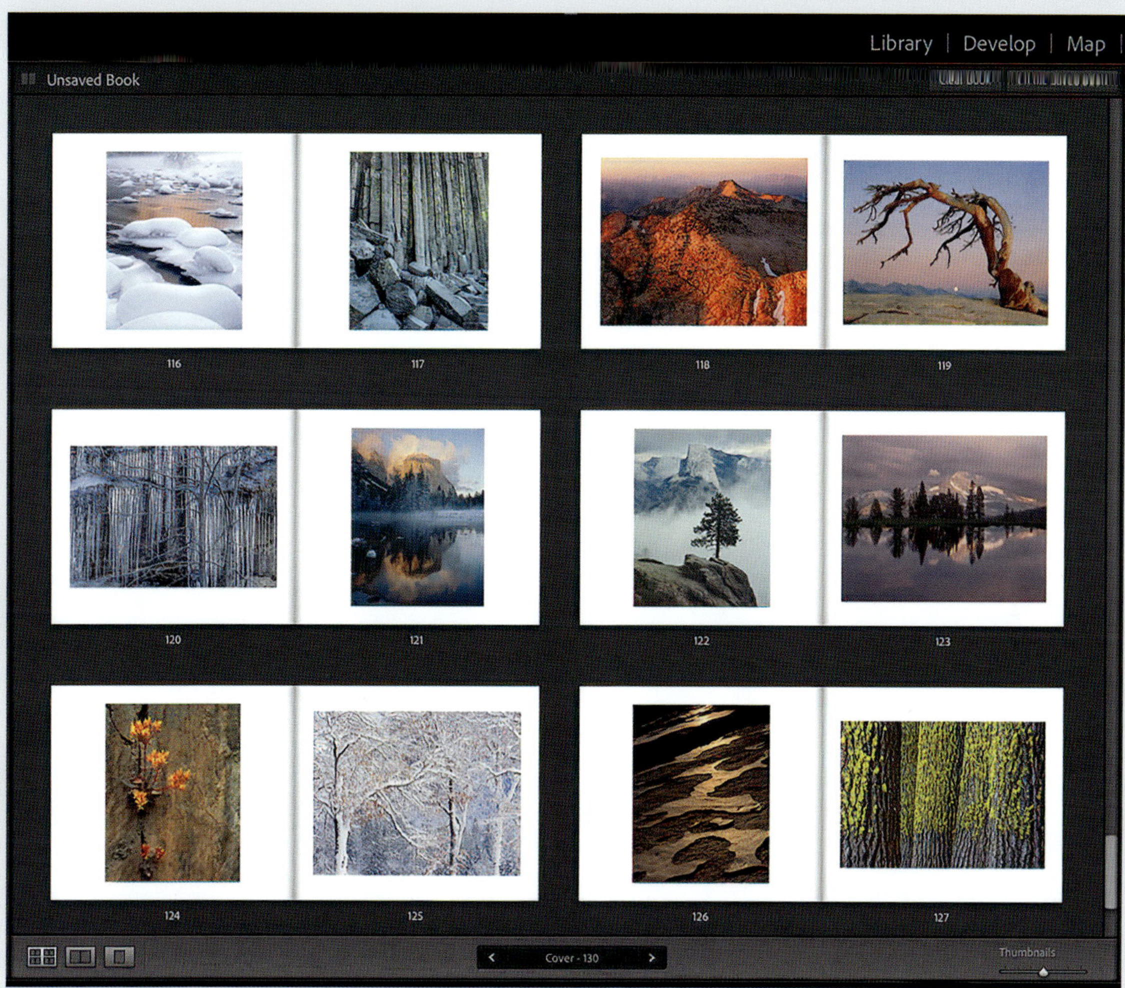

If you want to create a book, I recommend looking online for Book module tutorials to get up to speed. The information provided by Adobe's own Julieanne Kost have been helpful for me:

- https://jkost.com/blog/tag/the-book-module

- https://www.youtube.com/watch?v=ELkNLQ7uYtQ&t=159s

As you can see in the screenshot below, there are many control options in the panel on the right, including:

- The option to make a Blurb book or a PDF

- Book size

- Auto Layout

- Page layout options for single image, multiple images, text and image positioning, layout guides, and cell padding to control borders

- Text, type, background choices

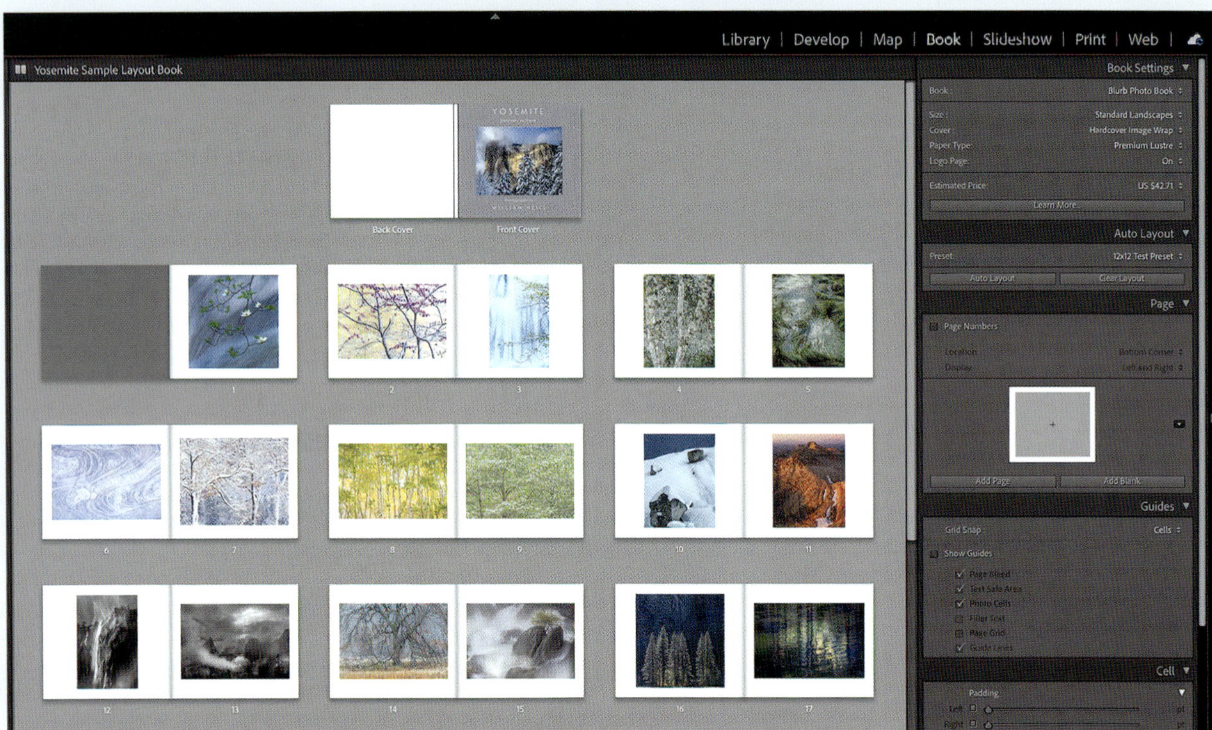

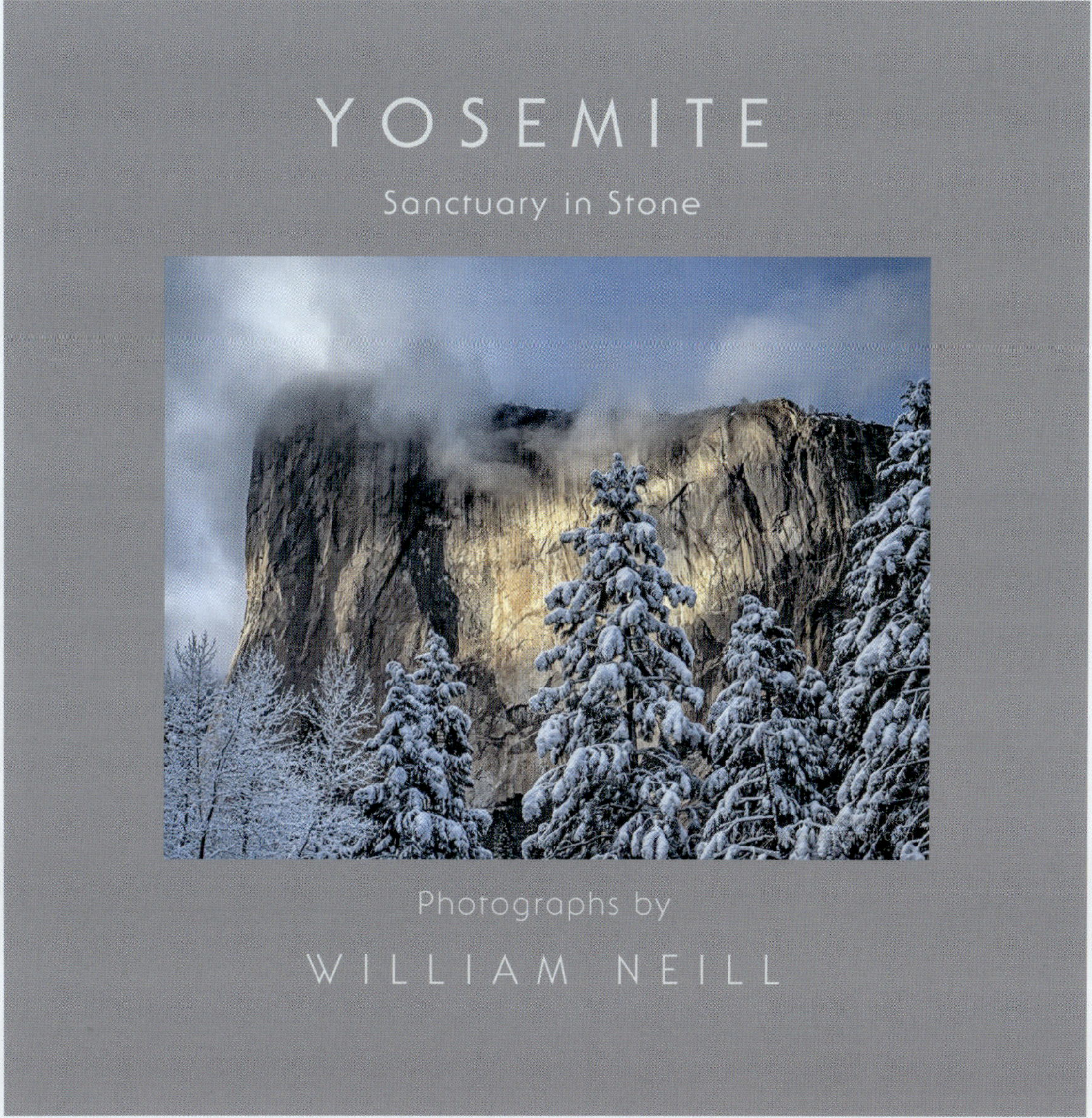

I want my cover image to convey a sense of how I feel in Yosemite Valley. Adjectives come to mind: protected, serene, grand, peaceful, magnificent. To show "sanctuary." This is my current favorite photograph that fits those words.

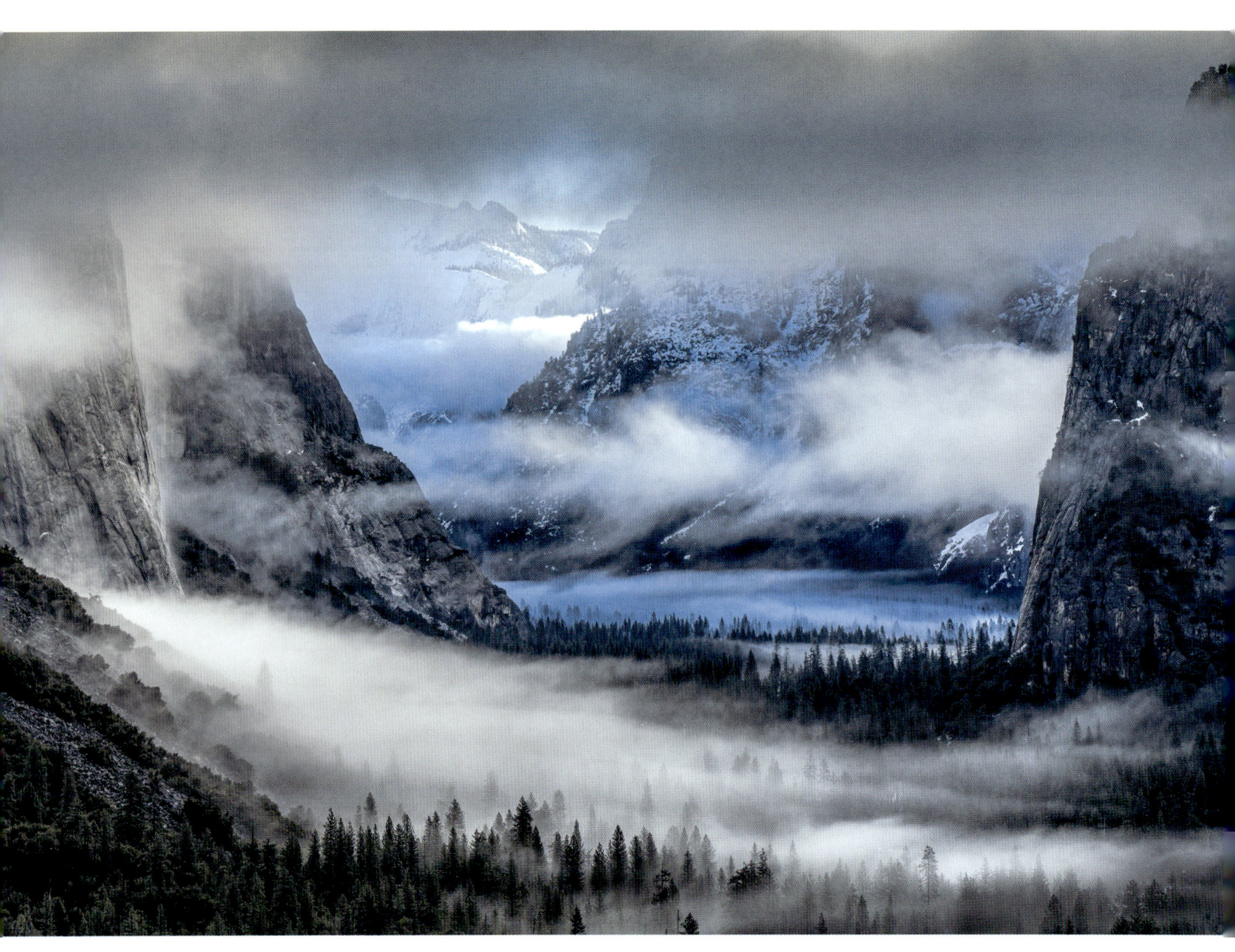

Shrouded Cliffs, Yosemite National Park, California, 2021

PUT IT ALL TOGETHER

OVERVIEW

The objective of Lesson Eight is to practice the realization of your portfolio by making your final image selections and completing your presentation.

ASSIGNMENT

Create your final presentation, which could be a book layout saved as a PDF, a web portfolio, or several other format options. (The assignment is described in more detail on pages 96–97.)

Let's start by summarizing the key lessons presented throughout this book.

Editing Basics

Quality control requirements:

- Check exposure: Appropriate for subject, mood?

- Check sharpness: Tack sharp where needed, DOF appropriate?

- Check the light: Is it special?

- Check the composition: Clean, clear, lack of distraction?

- Check the creative and emotional values: Emotion conveyed; your unique perspective revealed?

The Process of Editing a Portfolio

- Explore what themes you have in your files.

- Organize images based on a clear theme.

- Establish a standard of quality.

- Research other photography with the same themes that interest you and improve your visual literacy.

- Examine the possible contexts in which you might use your images.

The Feedback Loop

Feedback is vital for both editing individual exposures and curating a thematic portfolio.

- Benchmark (standard of quality based on existing work)

- New work

- Assessment

- Add successes to portfolio

- Reject lesser images

- Learn from successes and rejects

- More new work

Thoughts for the Journey

- Trust your instincts.

- Define and refine your theme and have passion for it.

- Focus your attention on the theme.

THE FINISHED PRODUCT

My dad had a saying: "Always keep a fluid front." In other words, be flexible. I have found that this attitude is very useful when it comes to gathering photographs into groups. When you build a body of strong images united by a concise theme, you will find many ways to use it. If you make a beautiful set of twenty fine art prints and place them in a custom portfolio box, you have accomplished a great deal. If you decide to make a calendar on the same theme, you will most likely need only thirteen of those same images. If you decide to make a book on that same theme, you may need many more, say forty to one hundred strong images. Each time you edit, the portfolio changes character.

Remember, flexibility in your editing does not mean sloppiness. Don't retreat from the standard of quality you've set for yourself. I can guarantee you that my dad did not mean sacrificing quality in order to be fluid.

My point is that selecting photographs for your portfolio depends on your context, and flexibility becomes a useful tool. For me, it's always a balancing act where I am considering how the images might be used. The struggle for me, and for many other photographers, is between art and commerce. Each photographer must decide what that balance is for them. Too many photographers give so much weight to the commerce side of the equation that they forget to make their art because their creative energies are used up making images that sell.

We all have photographs that may not be our most artistic but are of high quality technically and are worthy photographs that describe the beauty of a place or character of a wild critter, but they don't show unique qualities or artistic perspective. Do we throw those out, or make use of them?

I hope that this book provides those of you wishing to market and sell your work with some ideas and experience editing and refining your themes. In any case, you will improve your photography by defining and developing themes about which you are passionate. By creating portfolios of consistent quality and a clearly defined theme, your creativity and unique perspective will be more clearly seen.

You will improve your photography by defining and developing themes about which you are passionate.

CONCLUSIONS

A strong portfolio is the culmination of all your hard work. All the parts should be related but unique, and their sum greater than each image alone. Developing a focus for your photographic sessions will help you work more effectively and expand the depth of your work. I hope that you have gained a better understanding of what you have accomplished within your past body of images, and how you can improve as you create new work in the future.

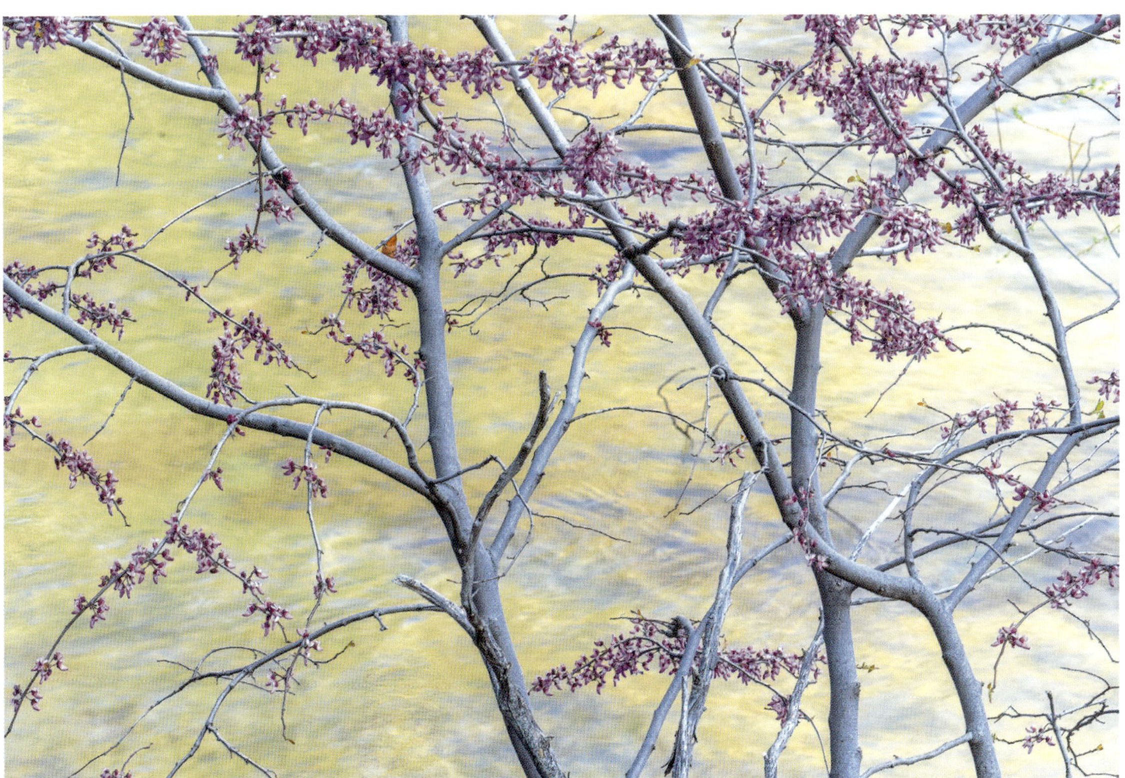

Redbud and Merced River, Yosemite National Park, California, 2021

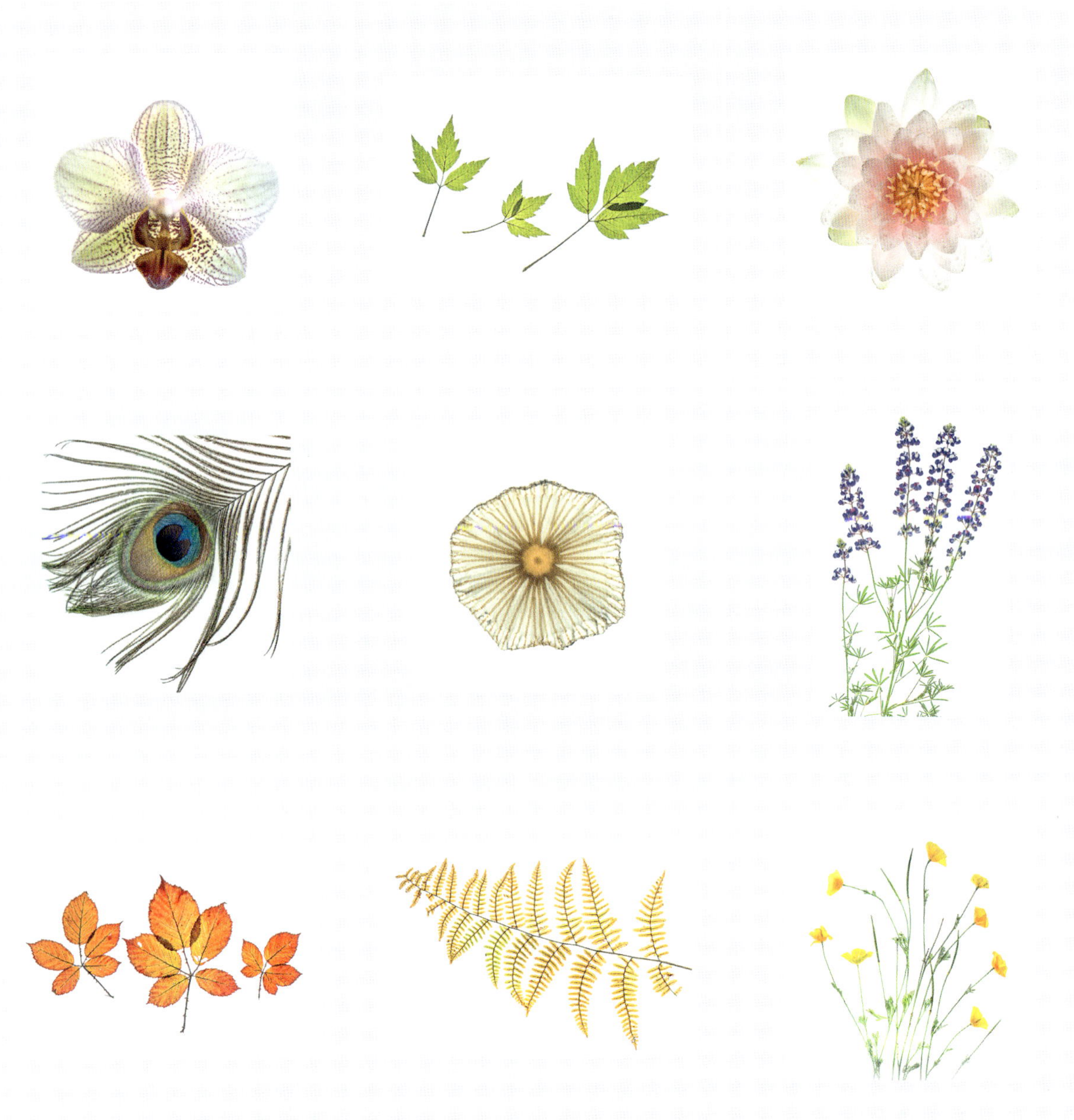

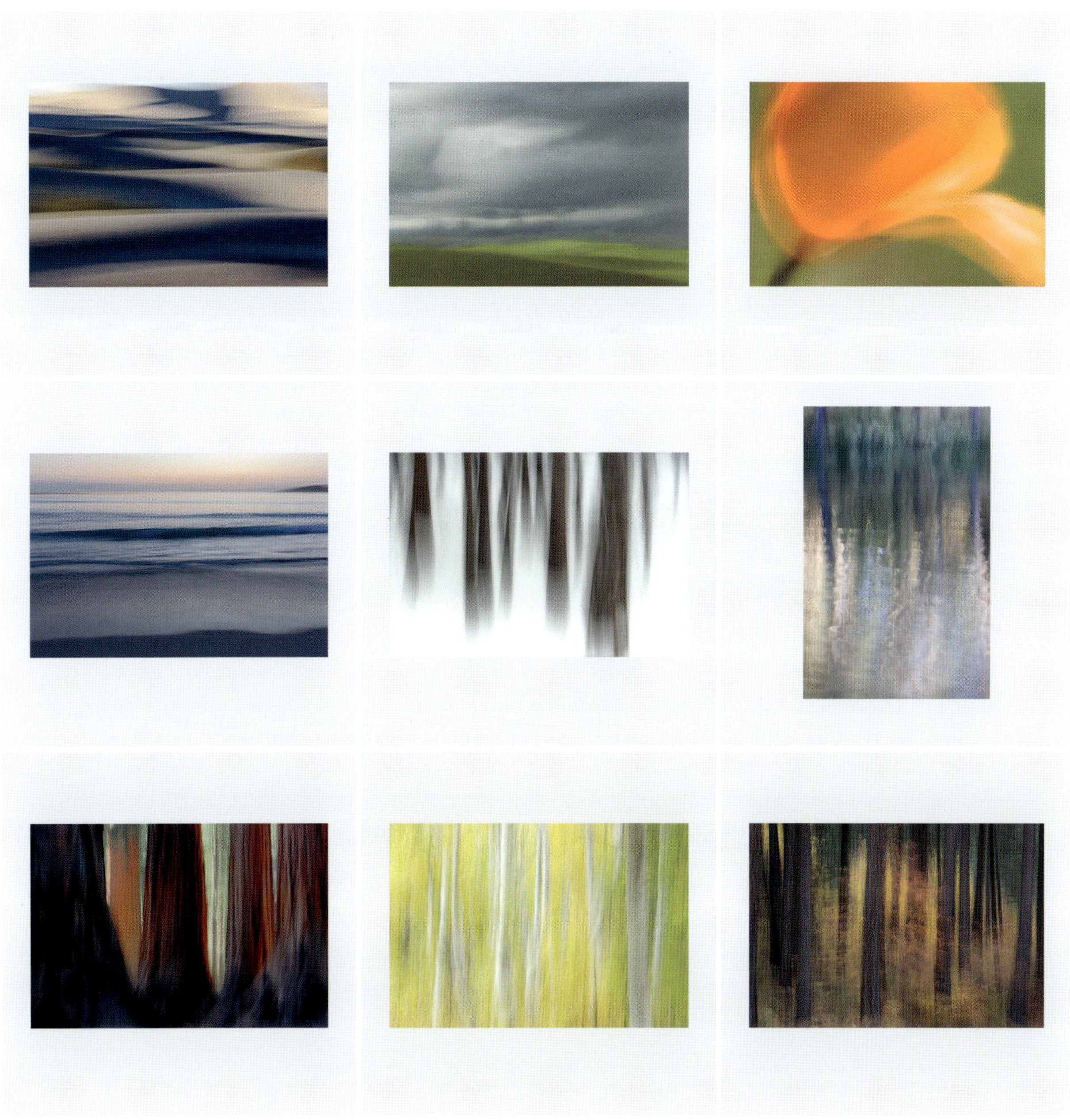

YOUR ASSIGNMENT:
PUT IT ALL TOGETHER

Now is the time to pull together a finished portfolio, which should represent your best work on a given theme. The first part of the process was for you to make the final selection of your theme. The assignment for Lesson Eight is the practical application to share your final choices presented in your selected context.

By now, you should have selected a context for which your portfolio might be used. Now it is time to move from theory toward practice. Select a method for a presentation using one of the options mentioned in Lesson Seven.

Allow yourself enough time to research that method, including downloading software and perhaps finding a few tutorials on YouTube or via other educational venues to get up to speed with basic techniques. If you don't have the necessary software, many companies allow for trial downloads so that you can test out the product.

There are many options to explore for presentations, and you will be more productive if you don't feel rushed. The research, the experimentation, and the application of any of the portfolio ideas presented in Lesson Seven are exciting but time-consuming. Don't worry if you don't finish a perfect version. The resulting display of your images will no doubt be worth your efforts.

Writing about the process will help you clarify what you have learned and where you can go. Describe your presentation method, the context for the presentation, why you chose one option over the others, how you might use your presentation for sharing, promoting, or marketing your photography (if applicable), and how you feel the process of "developing" a portfolio has improved your work.

I recommend using the same set of selected images for parts one and two below. If your presentation choice will require more than forty images, choose those that best represent the balance and overall quality of the full presentation.

PART ONE

Make a final selection of up to forty images on your chosen theme. If you don't feel you have enough strong work, you may wish to organize the work by chapters or subgroupings.

Remember that there are two main requirements for your portfolio: There must be a coherent theme that moves you and motivates you, and there should be no one image that is of lesser quality than another.

As mentioned in Lessons Four and Seven, I recommend that you write a short essay about your final choice of images and theme. I've included an essay of my own on the following pages. One optional approach, which would be very good practice for marketing, would be to write your essay as if it was a cover letter to a gallery, publisher, or other outlet for your work. Your theme title and short essay may help you define what images to contain within your portfolio.

PART TWO

There are many options to explore for presentations, as outlined in Lesson Seven. I hope you had fun checking out the options. Don't worry if you don't finish a formal presentation right away, but it is important to finish the project soon while the whole process is fresh in your mind.

If you want to make a book, use Lightroom or use one of the online services mentioned in Lesson Seven. Whether or not you order a finished book, these systems allow you to lay out a book, deal with issues such as image sequencing and pairs, page style, type choice, etc. You can preview the book and save the results for editing or a future order. I made my Blurb books with Adobe InDesign, which offers the most design control, but there is also a steep learning curve to get started. I've also used Lightroom's Book module for one book project, and it includes a built-in Blurb option for your convenience.

You could design a template for portfolio pages, note cards, or a poster series. Choose a standard paper size—such as 8.5x11, 8x10, 11x14, or 13x19—and experiment with border sizes and colors. In Photoshop, you can use the Canvas Size tool to add your borders, and the Type tool to add captions or other text.

To turn a small portfolio into a slide show or book will require a greater number of strong images. Be cautious about expanding a portfolio without diluting the quality or adding distraction from the theme. One way to solve this issue is to broaden your theme and organize the presentation into chapters for which you have strong enough groupings, and then choose the ten best or so of each. An example might be an overall nature theme with landscapes, nature details, and macro photographs as chapters.

My intent with part two of this lesson is to help you make the first steps toward the completion of a real project, starting here with the necessary research and trial and error. To supplement your images, write at least several sentences describing what you have done and what you have learned, defining your context and experience. Hopefully you will have established a feedback system with friends or mentors. I save all of my explorations so I can come back to finish later. Often, my ideas simmer for months or even years until I find time to explore them more or the concept finally comes together with new work or a final refinement of that collection.

YOSEMITE PORTFOLIO CASE STUDY

My idea for the *Yosemite Sanctuary* book as a personal portfolio came together in 2006, but ultimately, the project was dropped by the publisher. My first Yosemite book, *Yosemite: The Promise of Wildness*, was published in 1994, but recently went out of print. The new book will be more of an artist's portfolio than a tourist-oriented gift book.

On the following pages is a mock-up of possible book layouts, as previewed in the Lightroom Book module, where I have experimented with groupings of images. These are followed by an essay about the photographs presented.

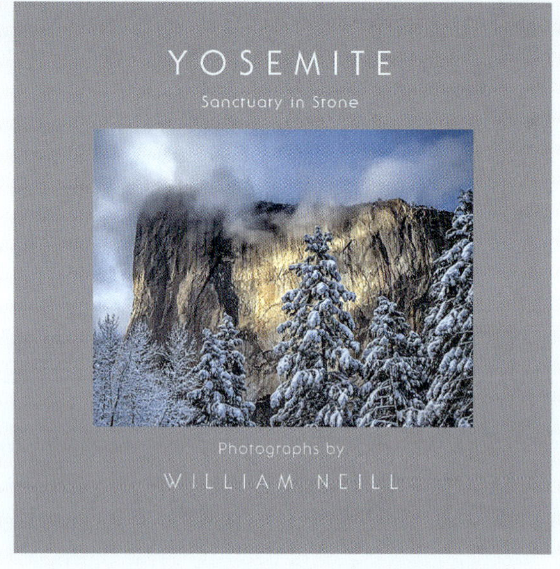

Yosemite: Sanctuary in Stone Book Cover

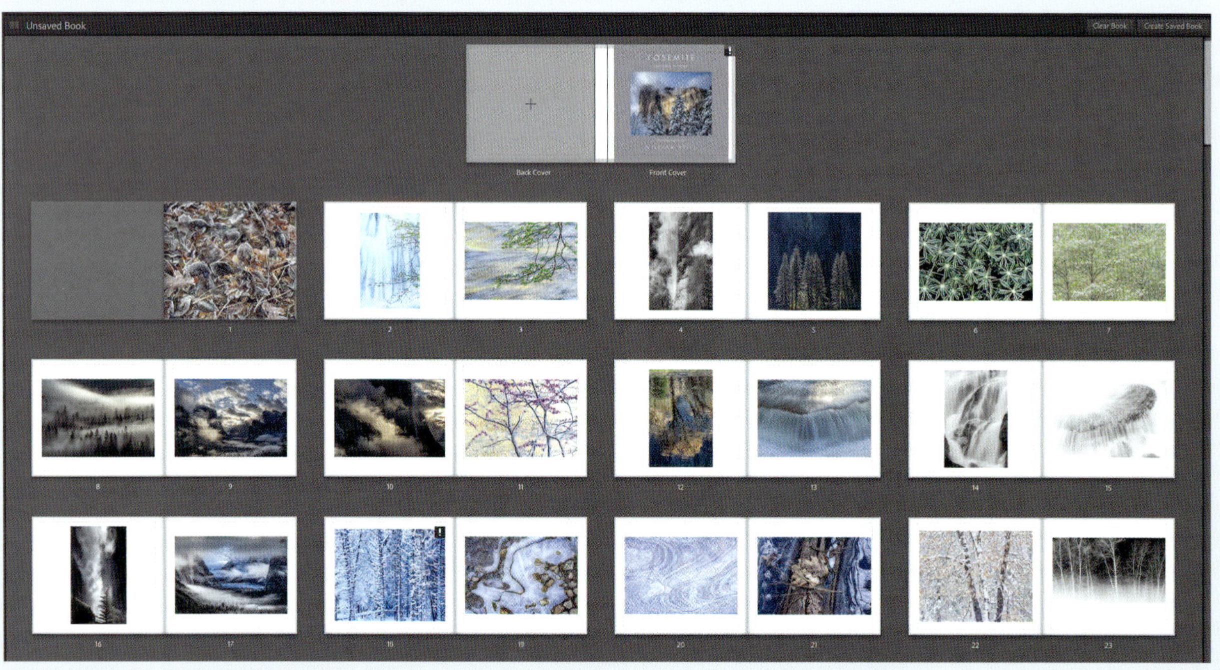

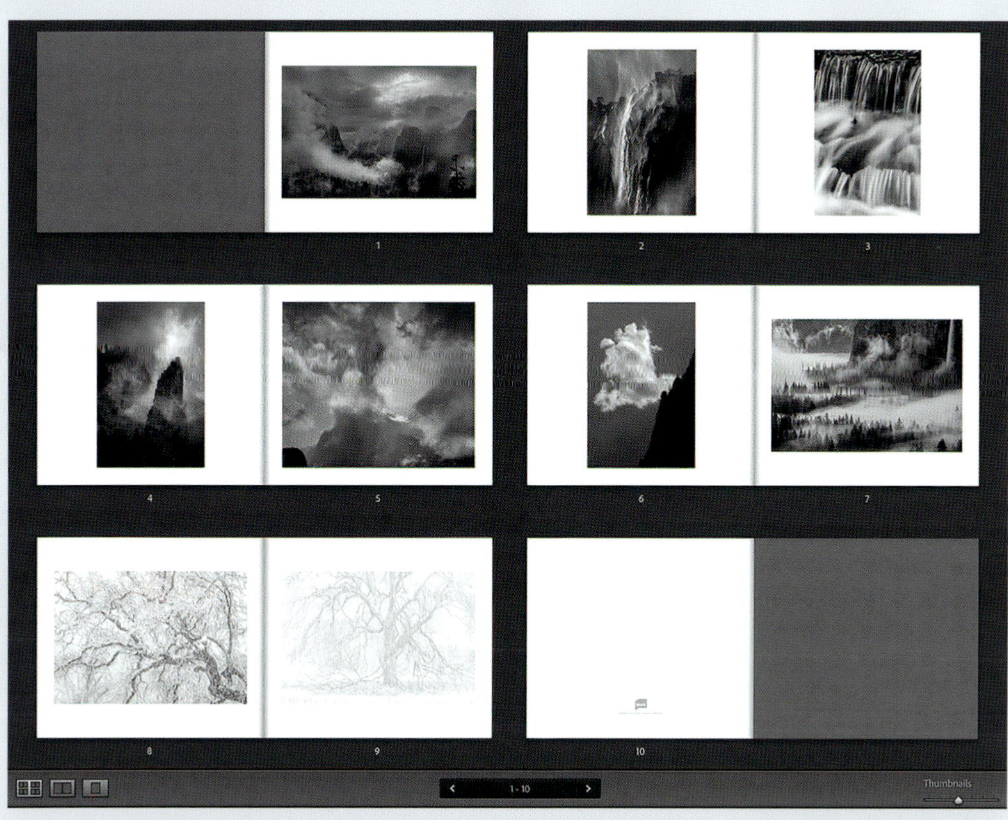

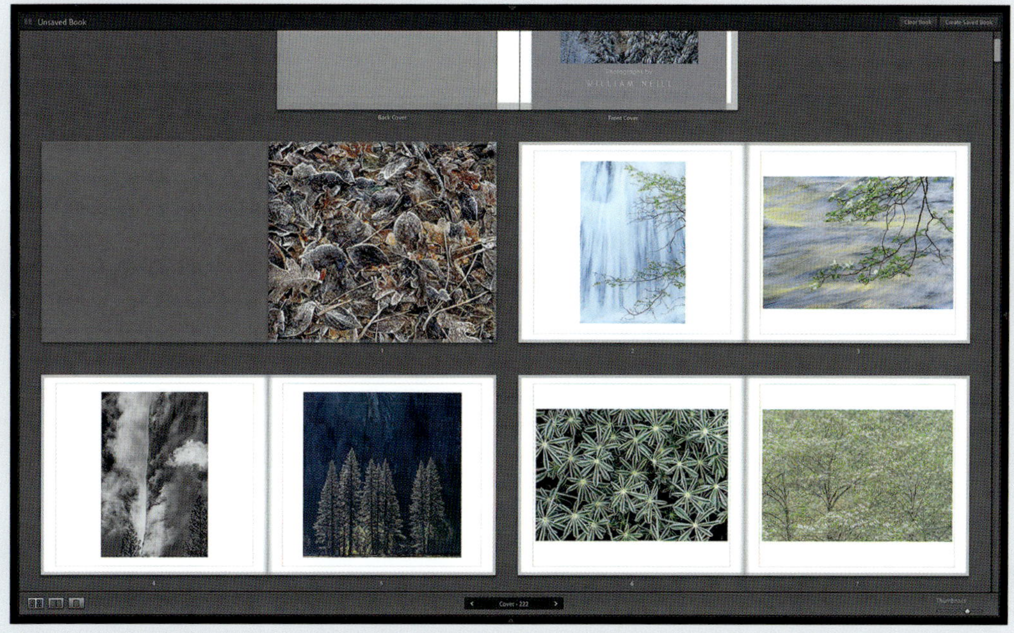

YOSEMITE: SANCTUARY IN STONE

In 1977, I moved to Yosemite National Park at the age of twenty-three. One year after graduating from the University of Colorado with a degree in Environmental Conservation, I had decided to pursue my passion for landscape photography in the Sierra Nevada.

I have now completed forty-five years living in the Yosemite area and photographing this famous national park. Encouraged by Ansel Adams and other mentors to pursue a unique point of view, I have attempted to pierce through the abundant clichéd views that appear at nearly every turnout, to convey my own vision of the park.

Living here has been an inspirational education, a mentorship taught by the landscape itself. When I managed to slow down to see clearly and listen carefully, I was able to learn many lessons about this landscape—its light, its seasons. I learned from missed opportunities, like arriving too late for the best morning light. I discovered that, in spite of well-planned timing, I did not find exceptional light or inspiration. Other times, I experienced magical light and weather when least prepared for it. I found awe and delight in Yosemite's grand and famous landscapes, but often I connected most deeply to its more intimate details.

What I've learned is that Yosemite, beyond its role as a nature preserve and place of recreation, is a sanctuary for the spirit. Millions of visitors love this place, for a wide variety of reasons. For whatever reason people visit here, they feel good here; they feel the restorative effects of wild nature even if only briefly. When I first read these words by John Muir, the resonance inside of me was deep and profound: "Climb the mountains and get their good tidings. Nature's peace will flow into you as sunshine flows into trees. The winds will blow their own freshness into you, and the storms their energy, while cares will drop off like autumn leaves." Few other words had ever rung so true to my experiences in these mountains. I came to see these mountains, inspired like so many by the images of Ansel Adams and the words of John Muir, and stayed.

I have often been asked how my vision has changed over the decades of photographing Yosemite. I may not be the best judge, but I say it has not changed. I have photographed the details of nature since before moving here, always finding small scenes that others might have missed. I still love the thrill of seeing, and trying to record, the grand landscape in epic conditions when they occur.

Preserves of nature, whether Yosemite or your neighborhood park, can provide a sense of protection from outside forces, much as do the walls of a church or temple. From within these protected walls, the peacefulness and beauty bring comfort and calm to me. Given this sense of sanctuary, my creative energies have been given the freedom to express what I feel, to express the connection between my soul and the beauty of Creation. I can't speak for others but this is what I have experienced. The lessons of Yosemite can be seen within all of my photographs, no matter the subject or location.

PORTFOLIO DEVELOPMENT WORKSHOP LESSON SUMMARIES AND WORKSHEET

The two main requirements for a portfolio are:

1. There must be a coherent theme that moves you and motivates you.

2. There should be no one image that is of lesser quality than another.

As you work through the process of creating each new portfolio, it is important to remember the feedback loop we discussed throughout the lessons so that you can monitor your progress. As I mentioned in Lesson Three, this process isn't always linear, but you will see progress. The practice, the repetition of the feedback loop, can be used on any theme and with future projects.

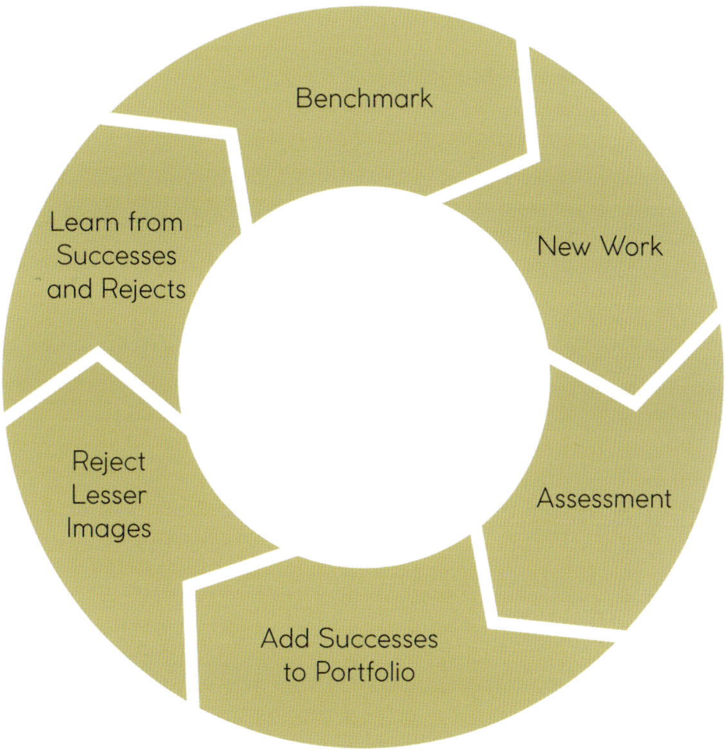

This worksheet is available as a downloadable PDF at: rockynook.com/portfolioworkshop

LESSON 1: FIND YOUR FOCUS

Learn what you have.

OVERVIEW: The objective of Lesson One is to begin to understand how to develop a cohesive portfolio that reflects your vision.

ASSIGNMENT: Identify twenty to thirty images that you believe are among your best and that comprise your favorite themes.

- What subjects or themes do you notice reoccur often in your photography? ______________

  ____

  ____

- What level of quality have you achieved with your past work? Consider both the technical and emotional qualities. ______________

  ____

  ____

LESSON 2: THINK IN THEMES

Edit for two favorite themes.

OVERVIEW: The objective of Lesson Two is to begin to organize your photographs by theme. This first step in the process will help you find your strongest themes. Then, once they are established, you will refine and build upon the themes with existing images from your image library.

ASSIGNMENT: Pick two themes about which you feel passionate and that show off your personal vision. Choose up to ten images that represent each theme (for a maximum of twenty images total). Being highly selective is key.

- Theme 1: ____

- Theme 2: ____

- Feedback from others or self-evaluation: ______________________

  ____

  ____

  ____

LESSON 3: EDIT ON A TECHNICAL AND AESTHETIC LEVEL

Photograph new images for one of those two themes.

OVERVIEW: The objective of Lesson Three is to photograph for a specific theme of your choosing.

ASSIGNMENT: Make all new images (not previously exposed photos) with a clear theme in mind, then analyze those images using both technical and aesthetic criteria.

- What qualities are striking in photographs that excite you? ______________________

  ____________________________   ______________________

- The subject I've chosen for this assignment is: ______________________

- Feedback from others or self-evaluation: ______________________

  ____

  ____

LESSON 4: BUILD UPON A THEME

Begin learning the process of building a theme from past and new images.

OVERVIEW: The objective of Lesson Four is to build upon a portfolio concept with research into your archives and by assessing what new work might improve the whole. We also work on the idea of "context" editing for specific uses or types of clients.

ASSIGNMENT: Decide on a theme, then curate your collection(s) using both technical and aesthetic criteria. Begin the process of writing an artist's statement.

- The subject I've chosen for this assignment is: ______________________

- Theme title: ______________________

- Notes for artist's statement (goals, adjectives that express what you want your photos to say):

  ____

  ____

- Feedback from others or self-evaluation: ______________________

  ____

  ____

LESSON 5: ADD DEPTH TO YOUR PORTFOLIO

Practice what you've learned to build skill.

OVERVIEW: The objective of Lesson Five is to focus on creating depth in your portfolio by adding more photos, whether these are newly taken images or photos pulled from your archives.

ASSIGNMENT: Choose one of your established themes and photograph specifically with that theme in mind. Add ten to twenty images, including two new images, that blend harmoniously with the existing images in your portfolio.

- Theme: ____

- What is the story line of your theme? What are you trying to say, and what subjects will illustrate your story? ____

  ____

- What new subjects might add depth to your portfolio? ______________

  ____

- Feedback from others or self-evaluation: _______________________

  ____

  ____

LESSON 6: REFINE YOUR THEME

Practice what you've learned to build skill.

OVERVIEW: The objective of Lesson Six is to continue to photograph for and refine your theme. With new work to add depth, you can expand your theme to thirty to forty images.

ASSIGNMENT: Choose one of your established portfolios and consider how you might improve it. Place up to thirty images on your chosen theme in your collection folder. If you feel that you have two possible themes, you can add a folder for a secondary theme.

- Theme(s): ____

- What other subjects or approaches might add depth to your theme (e.g., more details, more portraits, new location, different light)? _______________________________

  ____

- How well do the images in your portfolio blend together to achieve balance? This will depend on the goal or context of your theme; for example, do you want to include both literal and abstract photos, macros and landscapes, etc.? _______________________________________

____

- Feedback from others or self-evaluation: _______________________________________

____

LESSON 7: WHERE YOU CAN GO FROM HERE— IDEAS AND RESOURCES

Explore ideas and resources for sharing your portfolios.

OVERVIEW: The objective of Lesson Seven is to work on a specific presentation to practice the realization and presentation of your portfolio.

ASSIGNMENT: Choose the theme you wish to use for your final presentation. Add up to thirty images on this theme to your collection, including at least three new photos.

- Final portfolio theme: _______________________________________

- Working within your presentation concept, do you require any additional images to add depth to your collection of images? _______________________________________

____

- What presentation formats are you most attracted to? _______________________________________

____

- Notes to refine artist's statement: _______________________________________

____

- Feedback from others or self-evaluation: _______________________________________

____

LESSON 8: PUT IT ALL TOGETHER

Complete and realize your photographic vision and passion.

OVERVIEW: The objective of Lesson Eight is to practice the realization of your portfolio by making your final image selections and completing your presentation.

ASSIGNMENT: Create your final presentation, which could be a book layout saved as a PDF, a web portfolio, or several other format options.

- Theme: ____

- Context for the presentation: ____

- Presentation method: ____

- Why did you choose your particular presentation method over other options? ____

  ____

  ____

- How will you use your presentation for sharing, promoting, or marketing your photography?

  ____

  ____

- To supplement your images, write several sentences describing what you have done and what you have learned, defining your context and experience. How do you feel the process of developing a portfolio has improved your work? ____

  ____

  ____

  ____

  ____

  ____

  ____